Minnesota 101

Everything you wanted to know about
Minnesota and were going to ask anyway

**Kristal Leebrick, Ruth Weleczki,
Kate Dohman, Amanda Fretheim
Gates, Tim Lehnert, John MacIntyre**

MACINTYRE PURCELL PUBLISHING INC.

TO OUR READERS

Every effort has been made by authors and editors to ensure that the information in this book is accurate and up-to-date. We revise and update annually. Many things can change after a book gets published, and if you discover any out-of-date or incorrect information in *Minnesota 101*,we would appreciate hearing from you via our website, **www.101bookseries.com.**

© 2016 by MacIntyre Purcell Publishing Inc.
MacIntyre Purcell Publishing Inc.
232 Lincoln St., P.O. Box 1142
Lunenburg, Nova Scotia
B0J 2C0 Canada
www.101bookseries.com
info@101bookseries.com

We acknowledge the support of the Department of Canadian Heritage and the Nova Scotia Department of Tourism, Culture and Heritage in the development of writing and publishing in Canada.

Cover photo: Istockphoto
Inside photos: Istockphoto
Photo page 40: Paul Bunyan Land, Photo page 106: Sally Wagner, Photo page 248: Jonathunder

Printed and bound in Canada by Marquis.

Library and Archives Canada Cataloguing in Publication
Minnesota 101 [electronic resource] / John MacIntyre ... [et al.].

Issued also in an electronic format.
ISBN 978-0-9810941-8-2

1. Minnesota. 2. Minnesota--Miscellanea. I. MacIntyre, John

F606.6.M55 2010   977.6   C2010-904819-9

MIX
Paper from
responsible sources
FSC® C103567

Introduction

Minnesota is like interesting places everywhere; a product of its contradictions. It was our duty and pleasure to include as many of them here as we could, drawing what we hope is a portrait revealed one fact or story at a time.

As any of us who have lived here any length of time know, this is a state like no other. It is a sophisticated, salty, rural and urban mosaic whose lifestyle is often the envy of the country. This is a state that has a demonstrated appreciation for nature and the Great Outdoors. Indeed balancing that with economic interests has always been at the root of the yin and yang of the state.

No one book can really be about everything, of course. As you might expect, our toughest decisions were not what to put in but what to leave out. For every tidbit or profile or anecdote that didn't survive the final trimming, we gave a collective sigh of sorrow and crossed our fingers that it would make the next edition.

In the end this is a book about people . . . about Minnesotans and their view of themselves and the world around them. There are rock and roll and literary superstars, there are humble frontier men and women, there are political ground breakers, and, of course, there are the waves of new Minnestoans that continue to contribute and help define the future of the state.

Minnesota 101 could not have been written without dozens of collaborators and supporters, and so there are a great many people to thank. At the top of the list are the friends, researchers, and librarians without whose support this book might not have happened. A special shout out to Kristal Leebrick and Ruth Weleczki who carried the lion's share of the writing load, and whose affection for their state is evident in every detail. A thank you goes out to Jan Matthews who edited some of the book. Thank you, too, to Lynn Waters, Patricia Gladman, and Tracey Lothian for helping review final copy.

Finally, our gratitude goes to those whose personal takes on this great state were shoehorned into lists of five at our request — their thoughts and their willingness to share them truly helped us make this book unique. We hope you have as much fun reading this as we did putting it together.

Table of Contents

Hail! Minnesota

The music and original stanzas for Hail! Minnesota! were written and revised by two students at the University of Minnesota in 1904 and 1905. "Hail! Minnesota" composed by Truman Rickard was first performed on Class Day. In 1905, a second verse written by Arthur Upson, an editor at the campus newspaper, the *Minnesota Daily*, was added.

The official University of Minnesota song was adopted as the state song in 1945. Older generations of Minnesota children were taught the song in school, but many younger Minnesotans are unaware of it. "Hail! Minnesota" is being promoted again in schools.

Minnesota, hail to thee!
Hail to thee, our state so dear
Thy light shall ever be
A beacon bright and clear.
Thy son and daughters true
Will proclaim thee near and far
They shall guard thy fame and adore thy name
Thou shalt be their Northern Star.

Like the stream that bends to sea,
Like the pine that seeks the blue
Minnesota, still for thee
Thy sons are strong and true!
From the woods and waters fair
From the prairies waving far
At thy call they throng
with their shout and song
Hailing thee their Northern Star!

Minnesota:

A Timeline

2 billion years ago: The Iron Range starts to form as iron-rich minerals collect at the bottom of the inland sea that covers Minnesota.

1.1 billion to 550 million years ago: The crust of North America splits, creating a valley running from Lake Superior to Kansas. Minnesota is on the coast of the continent, near the equator, and plants and marine life thrive in the warm, shallow waters.

2 million years ago: The Ice Age sets in, with ice retreating and returning, flattening the land.

12,500 years ago: The most recent Ice Age ends. Glaciers melt into lakes and rivers. Spruce forests arise in open land. Giant bison, woolly mammoths, and beavers the size of large black bears roam the region.

11,000 to 9,000 years ago: People begin moving into the area, probably in pursuit of game. Hunted into extinction or unable to adapt to the warmer, drier climate, giant forms of life recede along with the glaciers.

Late 1650s: French explorers Radisson and Groseilliers meet the Dakota, whom they call "Buffalo People."

The Fall of the Dakota

The roots of the largest mass execution in U.S. history were sown with treaties signed in 1825 and 1851. After the War of 1812, the U.S. wanted to assert control over the Upper Mississippi Valley, which was inhabited by Indian tribes.

The U.S. negotiated three treaties with the Dakota-Sioux tribes. The treaty of 1825, as well as two signed in 1851, traded land for food and gold, and confined the tribes to a reservation, essentially a strip of land 20 miles wide in the Minnesota River Valley, stretching from the Yellow Medicine River to Lake Traverse. The Dakota-Sioux were supposed to get annuity payments of $68,000 for 50 years. The U.S. government didn't pay the tribes directly, however; treaty money went to Indian agents, who distributed it to the tribes. Oftentimes, these agents encouraged confusion, sometimes keeping the money as well as selling food supplies that were supposed to be part of the deal to white settlers.

Between 1849 and 1856, great tracts of land were opened for white settlement and the region's population grew 20-fold. Instead of outnumbering the white population by 2-1, the Indians now found themselves outnumbered almost 10 to 1. Moreover, when white settlers started moving onto reservation land, the government redrew the boundaries to the Indians' disadvantage.

Like many such wars, the Dakota conflict was fueled by confusion, double-dealing, misunderstanding, and smouldering resentment. The annuity payments were invariably late, much of the food was spoiled or stolen, and in 1862, with the U.S. embroiled in the Civil War, rumors began to spread that the payments might never come, as Washington was losing ground to the South. The Indians' geographic purview was ever narrowed, and hunger and hardship increased.

Treaty payments did finally arrive in St. Paul on Aug. 16, 1862, but by then it was too late. Dakota-Sioux warriors had killed four settlers that day, robbing them of their food. In the six weeks that followed, more than 600 American settlers were killed in a series of raids. By late September, the U.S. Army had, in response, forced the surrender of the Sioux.

Two months later, 303 Dakota-Sioux warriors were convicted by military tribunal of murder and rape. President Lincoln reviewed the trial transcripts and commuted the sentence of 264 Sioux (one was later granted clemency), but still sent 38 men to the gallows.

The execution date was set for Dec. 25, but President Lincoln is said to have held off the hangings until after Christmas to avoid dampening people's spirits. On a single scaffold platform at 10 a.m. on Dec. 26, 1862, in Mankato, 38 Dakota-Sioux warriors were executed by hanging, making it the largest mass execution in American history.

The remaining convicted Indians would stay in jail until later the following year, when they were removed to an Illinois prison for four years. More than one-third would die before their release. During this time there were also more than 1,700 Dakota women, children, and elderly men being held in an internment camp on Pike Island near Fort Snelling. They were subsequently removed by steamboat to drought-stricken Crow Creek in Dakota Territory, and eventually relocated to Nebraska's Niobrara Reservation. In early 1863, US Congress declared all previous treaties with the Dakota null and void, and began the groundwork necessary to expel the Dakota people entirely from Minnesota.

Late 1660s: Europe becomes aware of Minnesota through Claude Allouez's maps of Lake Superior.

1671: Sieur de La Salle asserts France's claim to territory around the Great Lakes.

1673: Explorers Louis Joliet and Father Jacques Marquette are dispatched from Quebec and are the first Europeans to explore the "Mechassipi," later known as the Mississippi.

1680: Father Louis Hennepin discovers and names the Falls of St. Anthony (located on the Mississippi in what is now Minneapolis).

1763: Treaty of Paris results in Great Britain assuming control of much of North America east of the Mississippi with Spain retaining control of lands west of the Mississippi.

1783: The newly formed United States now controls Minnesota's eastern half.

1803: The Louisiana Purchase transfers land from France to the new United States government. The land acquired includes the western portion of what is now Minnesota.

1805-06: Zebulon M. Pike, on behalf of President Jefferson, takes formal possession of Minnesota for the United States.

1818: The U.S. and Britain establish Minnesota's northern boundary at the 49th parallel.

1819: Lieutenant-Colonel Henry Leavenworth establishes a military post where the Mississippi and Minnesota rivers meet.

Bio Henry Hastings Sibley, the First Governor of Minnesota

Minnesota's first governor was Detroit-born fur trader Henry Hastings Sibley (1811-1891). Sibley, the well-educated son of a Michigan Supreme Court judge, had a love for the outdoors and, as an 18-year-old, he sought and found adventure in the fur trade.

At first, Sibley served as a clerk in his home state, but by 1834 the 23-year-old Sibley was named head of the American Fur Company's Sioux Outfit at Fort Snelling. In 1836, he built the first stone house in Minnesota, near the confluence of the Minnesota and Mississippi rivers. The area, which lies just east of what is now Minneapolis-St. Paul International Airport, is named Mendota (Dakota for "where the waters meet") and was a center for fur trading with the Dakota Indians. Sibley built a respectable reputation among the Dakota, who dubbed him "Walker in Pines."

Sibley was more than just a businessman; he sought to transform the rugged outback of Minnesota into a full-fledged part of the Union. Minnesota was recognized as its own territory in 1849, with Alexander Ramsey serving as territorial governor. Sibley and others pressed for statehood status, and in 1858 Sibley defeated Ramsey to become Minnesota's first state governor. Ramsey assumed the governorship in 1860, but Sibley remained as the state's military commander.

Sibley was instrumental in crafting the Minnesota state constitution, and the stone house served as the first "governor's mansion." The one-time fur man also had great influence over the state seal, land grants for schools, and other public missions. His most lasting contribution, however, is the state's name. Sibley argued against calling the state "Itasca" (which later became the name of the county that comprises the headwaters of the Mississippi), arguing instead for "Minnesota," from a Dakota word meaning "sky-tinted waters."

After his political career ended, Sibley remained in St. Paul, where he was a prominent businessman, head of the Minnesota Historical Society and president of the University of Minnesota Board of Regents. The Sibley House Historical Site is located in Mendota.

1820: Fort St. Anthony is built and later renamed Fort Snelling, after Colonel Josiah Snelling.

1820: First tornado is reported in Minnesota.

1823: First Mississippi steamboat (the *Virginia*) reaches Fort Snelling from St. Louis.

1825: A treaty establishes a line between the Sioux and the Ojibwe and runs in a south-easterly direction across what is now the state of Minnesota.

1835: Severe storms on the Great Lakes; 19 shipwrecks, 254 dead.

1836: New Wisconsin Territory is established and includes all of Minnesota.

1838: New Iowa Territory includes western part of Minnesota.

1849: Minnesota becomes a separate territory. Pennsylvania Whig Alexander Ramsey becomes the first territorial governor.

1850: First census counts 6,077 people in Minnesota.

1851: Two treaties with the Sioux turn land over to the U.S., opening up territory west of the Mississippi. University of Minnesota chartered.

1852: Hennepin County is created with Minneapolis as its seat.

1857: White settlers at Spirit Lake are massacred by Dakota upset over an 1851 treaty.

1858: Minnesota admitted to Union on May 11. It is the 32nd state. Henry H. Sibley is elected governor, defeating Alexander Ramsey.

1867: Minneapolis is incorporated as a city.

1870: March blizzard in southwest Minnesota drops 16 inches of snow, marking the first use of the word "blizzard," a boxing term meaning a flurry of punches, to describe weather events. The U.S. Signal Corps Weather Service would begin to use the term in 1876.

1872: Charles Alfred Pillsbury starts the Pillsbury Company which goes on to operate the largest flour mills in the world.

1878: Congress spends more than $100,000 upgrading Fort Snelling; the post serves as headquarters and supply depot for smaller posts to the west.

1880s: Iron ore mining becomes a major industry.

1881: Fire destroys the Capitol building in St. Paul.

1886: Tornado strikes St. Cloud and Sauk Rapids, killing 72 and injuring 213.

1889: William W. Mayo and his two sons establish the Mayo Clinic in Rochester.

1890: Iron ore deposits are discovered in Mesabi Range. Minnesota's population hits 1.3 million, up from 781,000 just 10 years earlier.

1892: The state legislature offers a $500 reward for the return of five-year-old Mamie Schwartz, abducted from St. Paul in a highly publicized case. The police find her the next year—alive—in Superior, WI.

TAKE 5 PAUL MACCABEE'S TOP FIVE
NOTORIOUS GANGSTERS WHO
CALLED MINNESOTA HOME

Crime historian Paul Maccabee, author of *John Dillinger Slept Here: A Crooks' Tour of Crime and Corruption in St. Paul, 1920-1936* (Minnesota Historical Society Press), spent 12 years fighting the US Justice Department to obtain more than 100,000 pages of FBI files, wiretaps and prison records on Minnesota's most notorious criminals. He has been featured in the History Channel's TV documentary, "Crime Wave," and in three A&E cable TV documentaries on 1930s crime history.

Bank robbers, kidnappers, bootleggers, mob assassins—during the 1930s, they all enjoyed safe haven in the Prohibition saloons and brothels of St. Paul, thanks to hospitality established by corrupt Police Chief John J. "The Big Fellow" O'Connor. Infamous gangsters from "Babyface" Nelson and Al Capone to "Machine Gun Kelly" and Katherine "Ma" Barker vacationed in the Gopher State, but the five most infamous gangsters to call Minnesota their home are:

1. **John Dillinger**. America's most notorious bank robber, jail escapee, murderer, and folk hero; named Public Enemy No. 1 by J. Edgar Hoover of the FBI. Romanced his girlfriend Evelyn "Billie" Frechette in St. Paul in March 1934 under the alias Carl Hellman, leading to a spectacular shootout with the FBI at the Lincoln Court Apartments. His escape from St. Paul led the Society of American Magicians to give Dillinger its Harry Houdini Award. His favorite pastime in St. Paul? Watching Walt Disney movies like *Three Little Pigs* at the Grand Avenue Theater which is still in business today.

2. **Homer Van Meter**. Bank robber, machine gunner, and pal of John Dillinger who was spectacularly slain in an August 1934 shootout with St. Paul police just a block from the Minnesota state Capitol.

The white straw hat Van Meter wore during the shootout disappeared for a half-century, then was rediscovered — and is now on exhibit at the St. Paul Police Department headquarters, with little bits of Van Meter's blood and brains still attached near the bullet holes.

3. **Isadore "Kid Cann" Blumenfeld**. Minnesota's own Rumanian-born Godfather — society bootlegger, tax cheat, gangland-fixer, convicted white slaver, accused-but-never-convicted of three murders, and arch nemesis of Minneapolis Mayor Hubert H. Humphrey. His nickname, "Kid Cann," was bequeathed to him either as a fighter's moniker from the boxing ring, or because whenever shooting started, he hid in the bathroom behind the "Cann."

4. **Alvin "Creepy" Karpis**. Bank robber, kidnapper, jewel thief, prison escapee, and safe blower. When doctors discovered the teenage Karpis had a heart condition, they advised the shipping clerk to take up a less stressful line of work; Karpis became one of the most successful criminals in American history. He met the love of his life, gun moll Delores Delaney, while hiding out in St. Paul. He also found time to mastermind the 1933 kidnapping of businessman William Hamm for a $100,000 ransom and the 1934 abduction of banker Edward Bremer for $200,000.

5. **Edna "The Kissing Bandit" Murray, a.k.a. "Rabbits."** Holdup artist, gun moll and liquor hijacker, renowned for escaping repeatedly from prison in Missouri by scaling the walls like "a rabbit." Edna earned her "Kissing Bandit" nickname from forcing trucks filled with valuables to stop on the highway, and locking lips with the driver who — paralyzed by her smooch — would be immobilized while her gang stole the cargo.

1894: Forest fire destroys Hinckley and Sandstone, killing 418 people.

1896: F. Scott Fitzgerald is born in St. Paul.

1905: Minnesota State Capitol building, constructed at a cost of $4.5 million, opens.

1911: State abolishes the death penalty.

1914: Carl Wickman and Andrew Anderson open the first bus line between Hibbing and Alice, which will become Greyhound Lines Inc.

1918: Forest fire in Carlton and St. Louis counties kills more than 400 people and destroys more than $25 million in property.

1918-19: 2,700 Minnesotans die from the flu.

1918: The Farmer-Labor Party is formed.

1919: A Minneapolis factory turns out the country's first armored car.

1919: Minnesota ratifies the 19th Amendment, granting women the vote.

1920: A second flu epidemic kills 1,700 Minnesotans.

1922: University of Minnesota's educational radio station, WLB, is the first licensed in the state. A year later, WDGY is the first commercial radio station to broadcast from Minneapolis.

1927: 25-year-old Minnesotan Charles Lindbergh completes the first solo flight across the Atlantic, flying Long Island to Le Bourget Field in Paris, France, aboard the *Spirit of St. Louis*.

A Night at the Fair

The Minnesota State Fair is not so much a mere event as it is a happening. For 12 frenzied days in late August and early September, nearly 1.8 million normally reserved Minnesotans (and guests) give over to excess. They party, they drink, they eat almost anything (and that anything is almost always on a stick). They meander half-hurriedly about the 340-plus acre grounds with no purpose, and no intention of having one. It is play time, and the seriousness of the oncoming autumn (and winter) is pushed briefly away.

The Great Minnesota get-together represents a confluence of barkers, hucksters, and carnies, with princesses, farmers and city folk. It's as if a year's worth of living must be compressed into 10 days. Children and parents from around the state save and plan and scheme a way to get to the fabled fairgrounds, located halfway between the downtown areas of Minneapolis and St. Paul.

Agricultural fairs are a tradition dating back to ancient Rome. When Minnesota held its first territorial fair in 1854, it joined rural societies everywhere in offering farmers a respite from the rigors, vicissitudes and hardships of farm life. It is a collective exhale from eleven-and-a-half months of hard work.

Although Machinery Hill, once the largest display of farm equipment in the world, may have given over to lawn tractors, SUVs and other suburban implements, make no mistake: this is a fair whose roots still remain in the country. Pie contests, 4-Hers, and competitions are dedicated to showcasing the best beef and dairy cattle as well as the top breeds of pigs, sheep, goats, chickens, ducks, geese, turkeys, pigeons, rabbits and even llamas. These provide not only the backdrop to the fair, they are its heart and raison d'être.

The fair represents one of those decreasing number of connections Gopher state residents have to their rural roots, and to country values and sensibilities that are refreshingly different from those of the big city. Butter statues and Princess Kay of the Milky Way are only kitsch if you are from out of state and never have been before. At fair time, all of everyone is out to have a good time and enjoy the simple pleasures that Minnesota and its fair have to offer.

The MAYO

After a severe tornado laid waste to Rochester on August 21, 1883, local physician Dr. William Worrall Mayo and his family helped set up an emergency treatment center in the local dance hall. Dr. Mayo enlisted the services of the Sisters of St. Francis to tend to the injured around the clock, and out of the disaster came Saint Mary's Hospital.

In 1892, Dr. Augustus Stinchfield joined Dr. Mayo and his two sons in the family practice, building a specialty and a team approach that lies at the root of the Mayo Clinic reputation today. In 1901, another doctor, Henry Plummer, joined the Mayo practice, putting in place systems (shared records, ability to move X-rays and other records between doctors, etc.) that facilitated the ability of doctors to treat patients as part of a team.

As early as the turn of the century-word had spread around the country that something special was happening in Rochester and doctors began to arrive to study the Mayo system. In 1915, the demand was such that The Mayo established one of the world's first formal graduate training programs for physicians, the Mayo Graduate School of Medicine.

In 1939, William and Charles Mayo would die within a few months of each other. They had lived long enough, however, to carry forward their father's vision and to establish themselves and the Mayo Clinic as one of the pre-eminent medical institutions in the world.

Today, there are over 4,000 physicians, scientists and researchers on staff; 3,500 residents, fellows and students; and 53,000 administrative and allied professionals. The Mayo Clinic now has facilities in Arizona, Florida and Minnesota that treat more than one million patients yearly. The Mayo's economic impact nationwide has been assessed at $22 billion, $9.6 billion of that in Minnesota. Over 34,000 of those working for the Mayo Clinic live in Minnesota.

1930: Sinclair Lewis is the first American awarded the Nobel Prize in Literature. Lewis, author of *Main Street, Babbitt, Elmer Gantry* and other novels, was born in Sauk Centre, Minnesota, in 1885.

1931: A road crew uncovers the bones of the "Minnesota Man," which turn out to be the remains of a glacial-age teenage girl.

1933: Great Dust Gale covers Minnesota.

1937: Hormel introduces SPAM. The canned meat goes on to become a World War II staple.

1941: Robert Allen Zimmerman (Bob Dylan) is born in Duluth. He grows up in Duluth and Hibbing, and later attends the University of Minnesota in Minneapolis.

1944: The Democratic Farmer Labor Party is formed when the Democratic Party merges with the Farmer-Labor Party.

1947: Basketball's Minneapolis Lakers, formerly the Detroit Gems, are born. The team moves to Los Angeles in 1960.

1948: KSTP-TV in Minneapolis is Minnesota's first television station. Manufacturing surpasses agriculture as the state's chief industry.

1949: Hazelden treats its first alcoholics at a Center City farmhouse.

1950: *Peanuts*, the comic strip created by Minneapolis-born and St. Paul-raised Charles M. Schulz, debuts.

1958: Prince Rogers Nelson (Prince) is born in Minneapolis.

1959: The St. Lawrence Seaway opens, allowing oceangoing ships to reach Duluth.

1961: First season of play for the NFL's Minnesota Vikings and Major League Baseball's Minnesota Twins (formerly the Washington Senators).

1962: The first Target store opens in Roseville.

1963: Control Data Corp of Chippewa Falls designs the first super-computer, the Control Data 6600.

1965: Tornadoes in the Twin Cities kill 14 and injure 685.

1966: First Best Buy (then known as Sound of Music) store opens in Edina.

1967: The Minnesota North Stars of the National Hockey League debut. The team relocates to Dallas in 1993.

1968: Democrat Hubert Humphrey, a former Minneapolis mayor, U.S. senator and vice president (under Lyndon Johnson), is defeated by Republican Richard Nixon in the presidential election. Humphrey had been challenged in the Democratic primary by another Minnesotan, Sen. Eugene McCarthy.

1970: *The Mary Tyler Moore Show*, set in Minneapolis, goes on the air. A statue in downtown Minneapolis now commemorates the scene from the show's opening credits in which Moore throws her hat in the air.

1971: Voyageurs National Park is established in northern Minnesota near the Canadian border.

1973: The state ratifies the Equal Rights Amendment to the U.S. Constitution.

1975: A three-day blizzard kills 35 people and 15,000 head of livestock. Some roads remain closed for 11 days.

1976: Democrat Jimmy Carter is elected president; his running mate is Minnesota Sen. Walter F. Mondale.

1979: A Jehovah's Witness receives the first artificial blood transfusion at the University of Minnesota Hospital. He had refused real blood on religious grounds.

1979: One of the worst tornado outbreaks in recorded history occurs in late June when 16 tornadoes strike the state.

1980: Twelve players on the US Olympic hockey team (the Miracle on Ice) are from Minnesota. The team is coached by Minnesota native Herb Brooks.

1984: Minnesota's Walter F. Mondale is defeated by Republican Ronald Reagan in the presidential election. Prince releases the movie *Purple Rain*, as well as the soundtrack of the same name. The album spends 24 straight weeks at No. 1 on the Billboard album chart, sells more than 13 million copies, and wins two Grammy awards.

1987: The Minnesota Twins win the World Series despite having won only 85 games during the regular season.

1989: Debut season for the NBA's Minnesota Timberwolves.

1991: The Twins capture another World Series.

1991: The Halloween blizzard dumps more than 28 inches of snow on the Twin Cities, and close to 37 inches on Duluth.

1992: The Mall of America, housing a theme park and more than 500 stores, opens in Bloomington. It is the nation's largest mall and employs over 11,000 people.

1998: Former professional wrestler Jesse "The Body" Ventura is elected governor.

1999: Honeywell is sold to Allied Signal Inc. Four thousand jobs are lost.

1999: A powerful windstorm knocks down nearly 400,000 trees in the Boundary Waters Canoe Area Wilderness.

2000: First season of play for the Minnesota Wild of the National Hockey League.

2002: U.S. Sen. Paul Wellstone dies in a plane crash while on his way to a funeral in northern Minnesota, 11 days before the election in which he was seeking a third term. Minnesota's population tops 5 million.

2006: Controversial conservative Michele Bachmann is elected to Congress as a Republican in Minnesota's 6th District, which lies to the northeast of the Twin Cities. Fire burns 31,830 acres in the Boundary Waters Canoe Area Wilderness.

2007: The Ham Lake Fire in May is the biggest wildfire in Minnesota in 90 years, burning more than 76,000 acres. In August, the I-35W bridge in Minneapolis collapses into the Mississippi River during rush hour, killing 13 and injuring 145.

2008: St. Paul police tear gas and pepper spray activists and protestors at the Republican National Convention in August.

2009: Minnesota Supreme Court ends a 239-day recount by deciding in favor of Democrat Al Franken over Republican Norm Coleman in the U.S. Senate race.

2010: Target Field debuts on April 12 as the Twins defeat the Red Sox on a warm spring afternoon. In December, the Metrodome roof collapses under heavy snow and the scheduled Vikings football game is postponed and moved to Detroit. Mark Dayton is elected the state's first Democratic-Farmer-Labor Party governor in 24 years.

2011: A May tornado hits Minneapolis, causing extensive damage and one death in the north part of the city. A battle between the Minnesota legislature and the governor results in a three-week shutdown of government services in July.

2012: June floods cause $100 million damage in Duluth and northeast Minnesota.

2013: Same sex marriage legalized. The Mayo Clinic announces a five-billion-dollar plan to upgrade and expand its Rochester campus. Record breaking late-August temperatures result in 80 State Fair goers being treated for heat-related illnesses.

2014: Public schools are closed state-wide on the first day back from the holiday break in the wake of record-setting cold temperatures (the winter of 2013-14 ends up ranking among the coldest in state history). The Metrodome, which had hosted numerous sporting events including two World Series and a Super Bowl, as well as countless concerts, is demolished. The Metro Green Line connecting the downtowns of Minneapolis and St. Paul opens.

2015: Five Black Lives Matters activists are shot by four men with racist sympathies outside the Minneapolis Police Department's 4th Precinct.

Essentials

Origin of the Name: The Dakota Indian name for the region was *minisota*, or *Mini-sotah*. *Mini* or *minne* means 'water'. *Sota* means 'a sky filled with fleecy white clouds that slowly float by'. Together they translated as 'sky-tinted water' and described the Minnesota River when it rose quickly in the spring and the banks caved in, giving the water the appearance of a beclouded sky.

State Nicknames: "Gopher State": Political cartoonist R.O. Sweeney drew corrupt railroad officials standing in a cart being drawn by gophers, ridiculing the five million loan of 1857," solidifying the gopher name.

"Land of 10,000 Lakes" (there are actually 11,842 lakes greater than 10+ acres) was a slogan used to promote the territory of Minnesota to immigrants "Bread and Butter State" came out of the 1902 Pan-American Exposition, where Minnesota promoted its wheat, flour, and dairy products.

Motto: "L'Etoile du Nord" or "Star of the North." Gov. Henry Sibley added the motto to the state seal during his tenure, replacing the misspelled Latin motto, *Quo sursum velo videre* 'I want to see what lies beyond'.

License Plate: "10,000 Lakes." Minnesota's license plate bore no slogan until 1950, when it adopted its current motto.

Statehood: Minnesota was designated a territory on March 3, 1849, and admitted into the Union on March 11, 1858, as the 32nd state.

State Seal: Designed in 1861 by accomplished artist and Fort Snelling commanding officer, Capt. Seth Eastman, the seal shows a barefoot farmer plowing a field near St. Anthony Falls to the right, with pine trees growing beyond them. To the left is an American Indian astride a white horse and the sun on the horizon.

State Flag: Royal blue with a gold fringe, the center is the state seal, wreathed with lady slippers and 19 stars. Excluding the original 13 states, Minnesota was 19th to join the Union. The large north star represents "North Star State." The dates, 1819, 1858, and 1893, indicate, respectively, the year Fort Snelling was established, the year of statehood, and the year the flag adopted. Amelia Hyde Center's design was chosen from among 200 entries for the 1893 Chicago World's Fair.

State Capital: St. Paul.

Largest City: Minneapolis.

Location: Minnesota is in the Upper Midwest; it lies south of the Canadian provinces of Manitoba and Ontario, east of the Dakotas, north of Iowa, and west of Wisconsin and Lake Superior. Minnesota is the second most northern state, behind Alaska: Its Northwest Angle, a finger of land in Lake of the Woods, pops across the 49th parallel and can only be reached by crossing the lake or going through Manitoba.

Time Zone: Central.

TAKE5 PROPOSED, BUT NOT ADOPTED, STATE SYMBOLS

1. **State amusement ride:** Tilt-A-Whirl, proposed 2007.
2. **State beer:** Schell's Deer Brand beer and Cold Spring beer, proposed 1987.
3. **State candy:** licorice, proposed 1997.
4. **State folk dance:** square dance, proposed 1992.
5. **State sport:** ice hockey, proposed 2008.

Source: Minnesota State Legislature

Legal Holidays: Minnesotans mark New Year's Day, Martin Luther King Jr. Day, Presidents' Day, Memorial Day, Independence Day, Labor Day, Veterans Day, Thanksgiving, and Christmas. By law, no public business, including schools, can operate on these days. The state school board can decide to make Christopher Columbus Day a school holiday.

Area Codes: 218, 320, 507, 612, 651, 763, 952

System of Measurement: U.S. Customary System of Units , which is Imperial units.

Voting Age: 18

Drinking Age: In 1973, the legal drinking age lowered from 21 to 18; in 1976, it rose to 19; in 1986, it reverted back to 21, where it remains.

Did you know...

that according to a University of Minnesota study, 93 percent of Minnesotans wouldn't live anywhere else?

YOU KNOW YOU'RE *FROM*

- You've gone trick-or-treating in three feet of snow.
- You know there's no such thing as a "Snow Day."
- You know summer and construction season occur simultaneously.
- You know where all the women are strong, all the men are good-looking, and all the children are above average.
- The Elf Tree has nothing to do with cookies.
- You know what SPAM is, how it's made, and you still enjoy it. On occasion.
- You know that Iowa's Corn Palace is no match for Minnesota's State Fair Crop Art.
- You know what Eveleth's claim to fame is.
- You know where Lake Wobegon is located.
- You elected a pro wrestler to the highest state office.
- You know what the "Opener" is, when it happens, and what you do.
- You've witnessed real people enjoying chocolate-covered bacon.
- You know that Minnesota blazed the trail for butter sculpting.
- You know the Minnesota hockey mom isn't *that* kind of hockey mom.
- It is a sport to gather food by drilling through 18 inches of ice and sitting there until, hopefully, it swims by.
- You are proud your state makes the national news 96 nights each year because International Falls is the "Icebox of the Nation."
- In March, as a child, you've called your mom or dad at work to ask if it's warm enough to wear shorts yet.
- You have refused to buy something because it's too "spendy."
- You're a card-carrying member of both the NRA and the ACLU.
- You have apologized to a telemarketer.
- You have had an entire telephone conversation with someone who dialed a wrong number.
- You beam with pride when royalty or a Hollywood celebrity comes to the Mayo Clinic to be treated.
- You were delighted to get a miniature snow shovel for your 5th birthday.
- Your birthday was in April, and you still got to use the shovel right away.
- You know how to say Wayzata, Mahtomedi, Chisholm, and Shakopee.

MINNESOTA WHEN . . .

- You support the preservation of forests, farmland and wetlands because that's where you hunt deer, pheasants, and geese.
- You voted for Walter Mondale.
- You never had to rewind any part of *Fargo* because you missed some of the dialogue.
- Your town isn't being ironic when it plans a winter carnival.
- Vacation means "going up north."
- You know where the Iron Range is located.
- You laugh out loud every time you see a news report about a blizzard shutting down the entire East Coast.
- You understand, and can explain, illegal defense, the infield fly rule, and icing.
- You measure distance in minutes.
- People from other states love to hear you say words with Os in them.
- You know what Mille Lacs is and how to spell it.
- The only reason you go to Wisconsin is to get fireworks, to fish, or to buy beer on Sunday.
- You drink pop, not soda.
- You call highways "freeways."
- Every time you see moonlight on a lake, you think of a dancing bear, and sing, gently, "From the land of sky-blue waters . . . Hamm's the beer that's so refreshing . . ."
- Someone has waved you through a four-way stop even though they stopped long before you.
- Weather tops the news headlines. Daily.
- The Dairy Queen is closed from December through February.
- Someone in a store offers you assistance, and that person doesn't work there.
- Your town has an equal number of bars and churches.
- Your daily meals are breakfast, dinner, and supper.
- Your gas station thinks "full service" means filling your gas tank, washing the windshield, checking the oil, and being friendly.
- Everyone has a cabin.

TAKE5 PATRICK COLEMAN'S FIVE
ESSENTIAL MINNESOTA BOOKS

Patrick Coleman, a Senior Curator with the Minnesota Historical Society, has been with the organization since 1979. He has added over 100,000 volumes to the library's collection. Fiction and poetry are particularly close to his heart, and he lectures on many aspects of Minnesota literature. Here are his five favorite works of fiction about the state.

1. *Giants in the Earth* by O. E. Rolvaag, 1927. Critic James Grey wrote that "...the conviction is strong in the true believer's heart that when [the Heavenly Muse] finds herself in Minnesota, she wearily gets out her make-up kit and prepares for a lugubrious session celebrating the sorrows of the soil and the soul." No one celebrates the sorrows of the soil better than Norwegian American author O. E. Rolvaag, and there is no more powerful description of harsh pioneer life on the great plains of this region than this. I can think of no better example of how fiction can enhance historical understanding. If you do nothing else, read the last paragraphs of this beautiful novel. It is worth giving away the ending.

2. *Main Street: The Story of Carol Kennicott* by Sinclair Lewis, 1920. *Main Street* would be on anyone's list of favorite books about Minnesota. And for good reason! The town of Gopher Prairie (Sauk Centre, MN) is so iconic: "It was unprotected and unprotecting; there was no dignity in it nor any hope of greatness." Taught as a novel about the small-mindedness of small towns, it is, perhaps more importantly, one of the first great feminist novels. Carol asks, in chapter 16, "What is it we [women] want — and need? ... I think perhaps we want a more conscious life. We're tired of drudging and sleeping and dying. We're tired of seeing just a few people able to be individualists."

3. *Staggerford* by Jon Hassler, 1977. Hassler is spot-on in capturing the people and place of Minnesota. The protagonist Miles Pruitt teaches English in the high school he had attended in the town of Staggerford, loosely based on Park Rapids in north-central Minnesota. Hassler describes the believable but eccentric characters in the town with a grace, humanity, and humor that is lacking in so many contemporary authors; one reviewer pointed out Hassler's unusual ability of "making good people interesting."

4. *Northern Lights* by Tim O'Brien, 1975. O'Brien's first work of fiction contains his best descriptions of Minnesota, in this case the region known as the Arrowhead. *Northern Lights* is set in the fictional town of Sawmill Landing (somewhere between Grand Marais and Two Harbors), on the North Shore of Lake Superior. The novel is a psychological examination of siblings who work out their conflicts and bond while skiing through the wilderness lost in a blizzard. The story is yet another reminder that in Minnesota, Mother Nature is often trying to kill you.

5. *The Many Loves of Dobie Gillis* by Max Shulman, 1951. Shulman's Dobie Gillis is perhaps better known from the TV series of the same name that ran from 1959 to 1963. *The Many Loves of Dobie Gillis* was probably even sexist by the standards of its own time, but the references to local people and places will be enjoyable to readers. The stories are centered on the University of Minnesota, which, the author says in a note in the sequel, "is, of course, wholly imaginary."

POPULATION

There are roughly 5.5 million people residing in the Gopher State, making it the 21st most populous state in the Union. Minnesota stands between Colorado (5.3 million) and Wisconsin (5.7 million), and has about the same population as Finland. Minnesota's population is expected to reach 6.2 million by 2030 and 6.6 million by 2040. Eight of its 87 counties have more than 100,000 residents. Of the 853 towns and cities, 14 have over 50,000 residents, and more than 61% have fewer than 1,000. Approximately 73% of Minnesotans live in urban centers. Minneapolis has a population of 407,000 and is the state's largest city; it's followed by St. Paul (about 300,000 people), then Rochester (111,000), and Bloomington and Duluth (roughly 86,000 residents each).

Population Density: There are 66.6 Minnesotans per square mile. By way of comparison, there is one person in Alaska per square mile, five people in Wyoming, nine in North Dakota, and 11 in South Dakota. Iowa is a little less crowded than Minnesota, with 54 people per square mile, while Wisconsin is elbow-to-elbow at 104. The US average is 86.

Where the Heart Is

"Welcome to Lake Wobegon, where all the women are strong, all the men are good-looking, and all the children are above average." To the world outside Minnesota, that single sentence is their introduction to the state and the Minnesota sensibility. The man behind those famous words may be one the state's most famous living citizens.

Garrison Keillor is, for all intents and purposes, "A Prairie Home Companion." Although writer credits often tip their hat to such folks as Sandy Beach, Sara Bellum, and Warren Peace, it is a wink to the fact that Keillor has written large tracts of the show and has done so since its inception in 1974. The show airs on public radio stations around the country and is heard in the United Kingdom, Australia, and New Zealand.

Minnesotans of all stripes have opinions on Keillor one way or the other, often both. Senators may represent the state in Washington, but, like it or not, Keillor is Minnesota's emissary to the world. Sometimes citizens feel the emissary has gotten it terribly wrong, or that he's simply too powerful or, in that most famous of local traditions, sometimes he just needs to be taken down a peg or two. The relationship is such that Minnesotans have opinions on Keillor's marriages (of which there have been three), his choice of home and his relationship with neighbors, and even the courageous act of opening his own bookstore.

Keillor has been clear that Minnesota nourishes his soul, and provides him with his identity. He is a son of Anoka, and now his beloved St. Paul. He is clearly a student of Sinclair Lewis and devoted to F. Scott Fitzgerald. For Keillor, these authors represent not only what talent a people can produce, but more importantly confirmed for him that Minnesota was worthy of being written about, and that there was an audience for those stories. They just had to be told. And tell them he has, not only in his signature "Prairie Home Companion" radio show, but also in over a dozen books, a number of them *New York Times* bestsellers. He also wrote the screenplay for the 2006 Robert Altman-directed movie modeled on PHC. For all the awards, accolades, and national and international attention he has received, Keillor is home when he is in Minnesota. He famously said that some writers need to go away to write about home. "Not me," he said. "To write about Lake Wobegon, I need to be around Minnesota." In 2015, Keillor announced that he will be handing over the reins of "Prairie Home Companion" to show regular Chris Thile, but will continue to pursue his Minnesota muse in various forms.

POPULATION BY GENDER

	Total	% of state total
Male	2.69 million	49.7%
Female	2.73 million	50.3%

POPULATION BY AGE GROUP

- Under 5: 6.6%
- 5-19: 19.9%
- 20-64: 60.0%
- 65+: 13.3%
- Median age: 37.6 years
- US median: 37.3 years

Nobel Prize Winners

- Number of people awarded Nobel Prizes: over 850
- Number awarded to people with a connection to the University of Minnesota: 23
- First Minnesotan to be awarded the prize: Arthur H. Compton, Physics, 1927
- Most recent Minnesotan to be awarded the prize: Brian Kobilka for Chemistry (2012). Born in Little Falls in 1955, he received a B.Sc. from the University of Minnesota, Duluth.
- Number of prizes awarded to Minnesotans for physics: 6
- Number for economics: 7
- Number for chemistry: 4
- Number for medicine/physiology: 4
- Number for literature: 1
- Number for peace: 1

TAKE5 PROPOSED, BUT NOT ADOPTED, STATE SLOGANS

1. Land of 10,000 Petersons.
2. Where the elite meet sleet.
3. Minnesota: Where visitors turn blue with envy.
4. Minnesota: Mosquito supplier to the free world.
5. I came, I thawed, I transferred.

Source: http://www.surfminnesota.net/slogans.html

MATCHED
- Marriage rate in Minnesota: 6.8 per 1,000
- Marriage rate in the US: 7.3 per 1,000

DETACHED
- Divorce rate in Minnesota: 3.2 per 1,000
- Divorce rate in the US: 3.6 per 1,000

HATCHED
- Birth rate in Minnesota: 2.14 per 1,000
- Birth rate in the US: 1.38 per 1,000

DISPATCHED
- Death rate in Minnesota: 715.4 per 100,000
- Death rate in the US: 838 per 100,000

CHRONOLOGICALLY GIFTED
Over 13% of the Gopher State's population is 65 and older, and one in 50 Minnesotans is over the age of 85. By 2030, people over 65 will account for 19% of the state's population, and the median age will rise to 40.2 years of age. Ninety-five percent of older Minnesotans receive social security benefits.

Did you know. . .

LIFE EXPECTANCY OF MINNESOTANS
- Men: 77.9 years
- Women: 81.5 years
- Rank among U.S. states: 2 (Hawaii is number one)

Sources: Minnesota Department of Health, Minnesota State Demographer and National Vital Statistics Reports; US Census Bureau

RELIGION & WORSHIP

The first church in Minnesota was organized by Presbyterians at Fort Snelling in 1835, while the first Roman Catholic church was set up in 1841. Protestants make up the largest percentage of Minnesotans and the state is home to the headquarters of three national Lutheran groups.

A study by the Pew Forum on Religion and Public Life found the following characteristics of Minnesotans with regard to religious life:
- Belief that religion is important: 52% (US: 56%)
- Weekly attendance of worship services: 38% (US: 39%)
- Daily prayer: 52% (US: 58%)
- Belief in God: 70% (US: 71%)

Did you know. . .

TOP 10 RELIGIOUS AFFILIATIONS

1. Mainline Protestant: 32%
2. Catholic: 28%
3. Evangelical Protestant: 21%
4. Unaffiliated: 13%
5. Black Protestant: 1%
6. Buddhist: 1%
7. Islamic: 1%
8. Jewish: 1%
9. Muslim: 1%
10. Don't know/Refused: 5%

Source: Pew Research Center

TO YOUR HEALTH

In the annual list compiled by *CQ Press* that assesses and compares such factors as infant mortality rates, cancer rates, and health insurance coverage, Minnesota is typically at the top of the list nationally. Moreover, the United Health Foundation ranks Minnesota as the country's third-healthiest state (Hawaii and Vermont are numbers one and two). And, despite the bitterly cold winters, the Twin Cities regularly rank high as an active and health-conscious urban area, thanks in part to an abundance of trails and lakes.

Did you know. . .

that the first open-heart surgery and the first bone-marrow transplant in the country were carried out at University of Minnesota medical facilities?

TAKE5 FIVE HEALTHIEST
STATES

1. **Minnesota**
2. **New Hampshire**
3. **Vermont**
4. **Maine**
5. **Massachusetts**

Source: *CQ Press*

SCHOOL DAYS

Minnesota has always stood out when it comes to education. *Forbes* ranked Minneapolis-St. Paul No. 11 in its list of the top 20 places in the US to educate your children. In 2013 *Forbes* named Delano, which lies 30 miles west of Minneapolis, number one in its survey of "Best Schools For Your Housing Buck." Minnesota ranks fourth in the nation in percentage of residents holding a college degree.

Did you know. . .

that Minnesota sent more athletes to the 2010 Winter Olympics than any other state? In 2014, Minnesota was tied with Colorado for second place, sending 19 athletes to Sochi (California was first with 20). In both 2010 and 2014, Minnesota was particularly well represented on the men's hockey squad.

Did you know. . .

that among the 50 cities with the most workers, Minneapolis holds the number-two spot for the percentage of commuters who bike to work?

They said it

"I have no object and no interests which are not inseparably bound up with the welfare of the state."
— Henry Hastings Sibley, Minnesota's first governor, in his inaugural address

They said it

"[It is a] most miserable & uninteresting country" and an "out of the way part of the world."
— Zachary Taylor, who served as U.S. President in 1849-50, writing of his experience as commander of Fort Snelling from May 24, 1828, to July 12, 1829

MAJOR LEAGUE PRO SPORTS TEAMS

Basketball - Minnesota Timberwolves (1989-): one division championship (2004), and eight playoff appearances.

Basketball (women's) - Minnesota Lynx (1999-): four conference championships and three WNBA crowns.

Baseball - Minnesota Twins (1961-): eleven playoff or World Series appearances since 1961 when the team moved from Washington D.C., including World Series wins in 1987 and 1991.

Football - Minnesota Vikings (1961-): Twenty-seven playoff appearances including four Super Bowl and eight NFL/NFC Championship games.

Hockey - Minnesota Wild (2000-): five playoff appearances, including one division championship (2008).

Did you know. . .

that the Minneapolis-St. Paul metro area's 18.3 million annual visitors make it one of *Forbes*' 30 most-visited cities in the US?

PORT OF DULUTH

Duluth represents the cargo capital of the Great Lakes, handling 40 million tons of cargo and 1,000 vessel visits yearly. The city sits at the western edge of the Great Lakes St. Lawrence Seaway, and is one North America's top bulk cargo ports. Nearly 2,500 miles by water from Duluth is the Gulf of St. Lawrence, which lies off of Quebec in the Atlantic Ocean, making Duluth the continent's farthest-inland freshwater seaport. The "twin ports" of Duluth, MN and Superior, WI primarily handle natural resources, and are responsible for 11,500 jobs in the region. And it's not all hurly-burly stevedore stuff down at the docks either; there are Great Lakes cruises which will take passengers from Duluth to destinations including Chicago, Buffalo and Toronto.

UNIVERSITY OF MINNESOTA

U of M was founded in 1851, but a lack of funding and the Civil War hampered its initial educational efforts. The school finally got off the ground when state senator, and later governor, John Sergeant Pillsbury (yes, that Pillsbury) saved it from bankruptcy. The college enrolled its first students in 1867, and in 1873 two Gophers were granted the institution's first bachelor's degrees. The numbers have grown a little since then. There are approximately 68,000 students enrolled at the university's five campuses. Roughly 44,000 students are at the Twin Cities flagship, and the remaining 24,000 are distributed among the Crookston, Duluth, Morris, and Rochester campuses. The majority of those students — 44,000 — are undergraduates. The University of Minnesota has 16 schools and colleges, and is considered particularly strong in agriculture and forestry, chemical engineering, education, media studies, and pharmacy. The university has an 8.6 billion-dollar impact on the state economy, and counts 400,000 alumni. The university has over 4,000 faculty members, and *The Scientist* magazine ranked U of M Twin Cities fourth in the country for patent creation and innovation. The Minneapolis branch of the Twin Cities campus is divided into a "West Bank" and an "East Bank" separated by the

They said it

"Maybe it's our 'Lake Wobegon' nature, where we're not looking to crow about ourselves. There's a very active non-profit community here, a vigorous civil society and a lot of people who are very active. It's just been our tradition here."

— Robert Hybben, Donor Services associate at the Minneapolis Foundation, quoted in "Most affordable places to live well." *Forbes*.

Mississippi River. On both sides of the river, an extensive system of "Gopher Way" tunnels and skyways connects the various buildings.

HIGHER EDUCATION

The percentage of Minnesotans 25 years and older who have graduated from high school is 92%, compared to 86% nationally. There are 32% of people in the state with a bachelor's degree, compared to 29% nationally. The six-year graduation rate for Minnesota college students at four-year institutions is 63%. Minnesota ranks 13th nationally in six-year graduation rate of bachelor's students, between New Hampshire and Delaware.

Sources: US Census, National Information Center for Higher Education Policymaking and Analysis

Did you know. . .

… that veteran actor and life-long baseball fan Bill Murray is a part owner of the Saint Paul Saints, who play in the North Division of the American Association of Independent Professional Baseball? Murray is listed on the Saints website as "Team Psychologist," and his duties include "morale boosting and train spotting." The Saints debuted in 1993, and in 2015 moved to their current home, CHS Field in Lowertown Saint Paul.

Shorthand

When you say the word *Minnesota*, hold the o. That's the sound of the Minnesota accent caricatured in the 1996 movie *Fargo*, a nod to the sing-songy inflections brought here by the Norwegians and Swedes in the late 1800s. Not everyone in Minnesota has a Scandinavian heritage or that small-town musicality in their voice, but Minnesotans in general do tend to speak with long vowels and end their sentences with prepositions.

They also share a common vocabulary, no matter what part of the state they live in. For instance, Minnesotans don't just go to bars on Saturday nights, they eat bars for dessert, after PTA meetings, and at weddings. When they talk about a deep freeze, they're not talking about the weather. It's the freezer in the basement filled with Grandpa's deer sausage that he made last November after he bagged that buck during the Deer Opener. That weekend's also known as Widow's Weekend, when a hunter's wife just might head to the Mega Mall down there in The Cities to do some shopping, even though it's kind of spendy.

Here is a Minnesota Primer:

A piece: An undetermined distance, as in, "He lives down the gravel a piece."

Acrost: The sometime pronunciation of "across."

Bag: What a successful hunter does. "I bagged three ducks last weekend."

Bar: A typical Minnesota dessert, similar to a cookie but baked in a square or rectangular pan and cut into squares or rectangles.

Barbecue: A mixture of browned ground beef, onions, and ketchup. Known as a sloppy joe in other parts of the country.

Bean feed: A public event that offers food (usually some kind of bean dish) at a reasonable price. Sometimes combined with political fundraisers.

Big Paul: Paul Bunyan, the mythical giant lumberjack who rambled through the woods with his famous blue ox, Babe.

Booya: A hearty stew of meat and vegetables usually made in large enough batches to feed hundreds of people. Booya refers to the food and to the event itself, which is often a fundraiser for such organizations as a town's volunteer fire department.

Boulevard: The strip of grass between the street and the sidewalk.

Borrow: Used as a verb to mean lend. "Can you borrow me a cup of sugar?"

Boughten: Store bought as opposed to homemade, as in boughten bread.

TAKE5 KAREN LYBEC'S FIVE WAYS
TO DETECT A MINNESOTA ACCENT

Karen Lybeck, a lifelong Minnesotan, is a linguist and a language teacher educator at Minnesota State University, Mankato, where she lives with her husband and two children. She offers her insights into the state accent.

1. **The long vowel.** Instead of pronouncing *know* with a *w* sound after the *o* sound, Minnesotans tend to fill in the space where the w sound would be with more o. This is noticeable when a Minnesotan says *Minneso:ta*. (The colon represents the lengthening of the vowel.) You also hear it when a Minnesotan says *road* and *toast*.

2. **More on that long vowel.** American English has what is called a vowel-plus-glide sound. The glide is a *y* or *w* sound. We usually hear four of these, commonly represented in spelling with an *o* as in *most*, a double *o* as in *boot*, *ay* as in *day*, and double *e* as in *beer*. A Minnesotan would lengthen the vowel sound in these italicized words: "I was *goin'* to the store the other *day*, because I *needed* some new boots, ya *know*."

3. **That sing-songy intonation.** When most folks say, "I was going to the store the other day...," their pitch goes up a bit on *day* to let the listener know that there are more words coming. Minnesotans might go up higher in their pitch during *other* and then end the clause by lowering the pitch to where the non-Minnesotan ended the word *day*.

4. **Coming with.** Minnesotans are well-known for the phrase "Do you want to come with?" This unique figure of speech is probably due to all the German and Scandinavian settlers in whose languages this question is made with a particle verb. (*Kommst du mit? / Skal du være med?*)

5. **The lend/borrow dilemma:** "Borrowed" German and Scandinavian words may perplex outsiders. This includes our somewhat confused use of *lend* and borrow. For example, it's not unusual to hear *Can you borrow me a dollar?* I suspect the confusion comes from the Scandinavian cognate, *låne*, which means both *lend* and *borrow*.

Brat (rhymes with caught): A bratwurst; a kind of sausage.

Cheeseheads: Wisconsin residents.

Choppers: Mittens made of leather with woolen inserts.

The Cities: The Minneapolis-St. Paul metropolitan area.

Cabin: A vacation home — no matter how large — usually near a lake.

Could be worse: Universal form of answering any kind of question that asks how a person is doing. No matter how things are, they could always be worse.

Cow pie: Dried cow manure left by the bovines in the pastures of a dairy farm.

Croppie: Minnesota name for the panfish everybody else calls crappie.

Deep freeze: A freezer chest that Minnesotans keep either in their basements or garages.

Deer Opener: Opening day of deer season. Also called "Widow's Weekend" for obvious reasons. In 2003, then-governor Tim Pawlenty, an avid hunter, established the "Governors' Deer Hunting Opener" in which the state's top politician kicks off the season and presides over a celebration of deer hunting in the state.

DFL: The Democratic-Farmer-Labor Party of Minnesota, formed in 1944 when the Minnesota Democratic and Farmer-Labor parties merged.

TAKE5 HOWARD MOHR'S FIVE WAYS
EVEN YOU CAN TALK LIKE A MINNESOTAN

Howard Mohr, author of *How to Talk Minnesotan*, which was originally published in 1987, is a former English professor at Southwest Minnesota State University. Mohr wrote for *A Prairie Home Companion* in its early years, and the commercials he created for the fictional Minnesota Language Systems ("the simple cassette-tape and study guide for visitors from out of state, so they don't stick out like a sore thumb") became the heart of his book. Since its publication, *How to Talk Minnesotan* has been made into a musical and television special. In 2013, a new edition was published ("Revised for the 21st Century). Says Mohr: "You can get along with anybody using these tips . . . if you speak only when spoken to."

1. **"You bet."** Often used in response to "thank you" or "I appreciate it." It can also be used as a response to a question when you can't think of anything else to say. It's meant to be agreeable and doesn't obligate the speaker to a strong position on a topic.

2. **"That's different."** Using this phrase means you do have an opinion but you're holding back the details. A Minnesotan visiting the Walker Art Center in Minneapolis may say, "That's different" when commenting on a piece of art.

3. **"Whatever."** Expresses emotional turmoil when "you bet" and "that's different" won't do the job. If the company president says, "You've worked here for 20 years, Bob, but we're gonna let you go. It's the economy." Bob would say, "Whatever." No use going overboard.

4. **Express the positive by using the negative.** It's okay to have good feelings, but there's no sense running down the street telling people about it at the top of your voice. There's a good chance it won't last, anyway.

5. **Use indirect speech.** Minnesotans like to avoid confrontation, particularly in conversation. They do this by making indirect commands and statements. A popular form of indirect speech — especially for men — is using third-person rather than using "I." A Minnesota man who's been asked about how he would repair a leaking toilet might say, "Well, I think if a guy took off that float valve with vice grips, he could maybe get at the gasket then."

TAKE 5 FIVE QUICK
OLE AND LENA QUIPS

Ole and Lena are characters in jokes told by Scandinavian-Americans. In Minnesota it is often a conversation starter, a potential prelude to a longer discussion about the weather. Lena is brighter than Ole, and she is forever explaining Ole's misadventures, usually with a faux Scandinavian accent. The two Norwegian characters are sometimes joined by Lars or Sven . . . who, believe it or not, are not quite as bright as Ole.

1. When Ole and Lena were young and in love they would go to their favorite spot to park. One night while hugging and kissing, Ole asks Lena, "Lena, how would you like to go in the back?" "No," she replies. So they hug and kiss some more. Again, Ole asks Lena to go in the back. Lena replies, "Ole, why are you always asking me to go in the back? I want to stay in front with you!"

2. Ole and Lena got married. On their honeymoon trip they were nearing Minneapolis when Ole put his hand on Lena's knee. Giggling, Lena said, "Ole, you can go farther if ya vant to," so Ole drove to Duluth.

3. Ole and Lars were on their very first train ride, heading from Hinckley to Minneapolis. They had brought along bananas for lunch. Just as they began to peel them, the train entered a long, dark tunnel. "Have you eaten your banana yet?" Ole asked excitedly. "No," replied Lars. "Vell don't touch it den," Ole exclaimed. "I yust took vun bite and vent blind!"

4. Lena called the airlines information desk and inquired, "How long does it take to fly from Minneapolis to Fargo?" "Just a minute," said the busy clerk. "Vell," said Lena, "if it has to go dat fast, I tink I'll just take da bus."

5. Ole and Lars went fishing in Canada and returned with only one fish. "The way I figger it, dat fish cost us $400," said Lars. "Vell," said Ole, "at dat price it's a good ting ve didn't catch any more."

TAKE5 SLANG PECULIARITIES

1. Minnesotans frequently end their sentences with "**with**," as in "Are you coming with?" rather than "Are you coming with me?"

2. The word "**then**" is often heard at the end of a question: "Are you going to town, then?"

3. "**Don't you know**" is another phrase that can end a Minnesota sentence, but it's often pronounced "dontchaknow:" "They're having a baby, dontchaknow."

4. Minnesota children play "**Duck, Duck, Gray Duck**" rather than "Duck, Duck, Goose."

5. "**Oh, for**" is what Minnesotans use when they are incredulous: "Oh, for Pete's sake." "Oh, for, cute." "Oh, for crying out loud."

Dinner: The main meal of the day, which often is the midday meal. See "lunch."

Din't: Contraction of the contraction *didn't*. Minnesotans drop the second d.

Dulut: How Minnesotans pronounce Duluth, a city on Lake Superior.

Fish house: A shanty or shack on a frozen lake that provides shelter while ice fishing. Can be a plastic tarp draped over 2x4s or a fancy structure with heat, bunks, electricity, and cooking facilities.

For cute: An explanation said when something is pleasing. "Oh, for cute."

For sure: A phrase that means the speaker agrees with the person they are talking to. First speaker: "The governor's an idiot." Second speaker: "For sure."

In St. Paul public schools, the largest school district in the state, some 15,772 students — or 41% of the student body — are not native English speakers. Students there speak 126 languages and dialects. The top 5:

1. **English:** 21,775
2. **Hmong:** 9,658
3. **Spanish:** 4,194
4. **Somali:** 885
5. **Burmese/Karen:** 627

Source: ELL Fact Sheet, St. Paul Public Schools.

Froze up: When something stops working. "My car/computer/washing machine froze up."

Give a ring: To call someone on the telephone.

Give it here: Hand it to me.

Gravel: An unpaved but graveled road. "He flew in the Mustang down the gravel."

Great Minnesota Get-Together: The Minnesota State Fair, which runs for 12 days starting in August and ending on Labor Day.

Greater Minnesota: A term sometimes used to refer to "outstate" Minnesota. See "outstate."

Heckuva: A really great thing. "A heckuva weekend."

Homer Hanky: A handkerchief printed with a baseball-shaped logo during the Minnesota Twins championship seasons.

Hotdish: A main course baked and served in a single dish. Usually combines canned soups and vegetables, meat, and a starch like potatoes or noodles (sometimes potato chips).

Ice dam: A ridge of ice that forms at the edge of a roof and prevents snowmelt from running off. The water backs up behind the dam and can leak into a home, causing damage to walls, ceilings, insulation.

Iron Range: Also called "The Range," it's an area in the northeastern section of the state that has distinct bands of iron deposits.

Ishda: Something that is icky. "That lutefisk looks pretty ishda!"

Jobbies: A small number of items or objects needed to put something together.

Jump: What a neighbor gives you, via jumper cables, when your car battery has died — a common event during Minnesota winters.

Leave it go: Let it go. Step away.

Lunch: Similar to a snack, lunch can be eaten a number of times a day in Minnesota. Commonly consists of a drink, meat sandwiches on small buns, and bars. See "dinner."

Long Johns: Rectangular-shaped pastries filled with pudding. Also full-length winter underwear.

Lutefisk: A traditional Nordic dish made of dried whitefish soaked in lye (yes, lye) that tends to be eaten by those of Norwegian lineage around the Christmas holiday.

MEA (pronounced em-ee-ay): A four-day weekend in October when all public schools close and the state's public school teachers' union holds its annual convention. The union was once called the Minnesota Education Association (MEA) but is now called Education Minnesota. Still, that October weekend is referred to as MEA.

Mega Mall: The Mall of America in Bloomington. Houses more than 500 stores, an amusement park, and so much more.

Minnesota nice: The behavior attributed to longtime Minnesota residents that includes being polite, avoiding confrontation, not wanting to make a fuss about something or to stand out, emotional restraint, and self-deprecation. Some people describe Minnesota nice as passive aggression.

Norskies: People of Norwegian descent.

Not too bad: An understatement which actually means pretty good.

Okay then: An expression of either agreement or resignation.

On-sale/off-sale: The two types of liquor licenses available in the state. On-sale refers to a license that allows establishments such as restaurants and bars to sell liquor for consumption at the establishment. Off-sale is a license that allows an establishment to sell liquor, wine, and beer for carry out by a customer.

Out East: East Coast.

Outstate: The area outside of the Cities.

Pank: To stamp down and pack snow to form a walking path.

Parking ramp: The building where you can park your car. One higher than one story.

Pill Hill: A neighborhood in Rochester that is listed on the National Register of Historic Places and has been home to staff of the nearby Mayo Clinic (hence the name "Pill") since the late 1800s, after Dr. William Worrall Mayo began his practice in the town.

Pop: Soda, soft drinks.

Popple: Aspen or poplar tree.

Pronto Pup: A hot dog on a stick dipped in a wheat flour batter and deep fried.

Rambler: A one-story house where the bedrooms, living area and kitchen are all on the same floor. Known elsewhere as a bungalow.

Sack: A bag.

Scandihoovians: An affectionate name for people with Scandinavian ancestry.

Skol: Norse word for cheers or a toast.

Sled: A snowmobile.

Snus: Chewing tobacco.

Sorels: A popular brand of winter boot that combines a leather and rubber exterior with felt inserts.

Spendy: Something that cost a lot of money: "That trip to the Cities was spendy."

Tad: Slightly, a little bit.

That's different: This is an expression that is an act of significant disapproval.

The Range: See *Iron Range*.

Three-two: Beer that contains no more than 3.2% alcohol by weight sold in convenience and grocery stores throughout Minnesota.

Tuque: Knitted winter hat, borrowed from French Canadians.

Twin Cities: Minneapolis and St. Paul.

Twinkies: An affectionate nickname for the Minnesota Twins baseball team.

Uff-da: A Norwegian exclamation that translates to "Off it!" In the family of terms Minnesotans use when they drop something or are exasperated: "Oops," "uh oh," "oh my," and "I'll be darned."

Up North: Where people go on weekends: anywhere north of the Twin Cities or north of wherever the person is at the time.

Warming house: Shelters built around ice rinks where you can put on your skates.

Went: Broke down. "That '89 Ford just got up and went on me."

Widow's Weekend: The weekend in November when deer hunting season opens and hunters head to the woods.

Winter survival kit: Things people keep in their cars during the winter in case they drive into a ditch or are stranded in a snowstorm. Items include blankets, a first-aid kit, nonperishable food such as granola bars or crackers, strike-anywhere matches in a water-tight container, candles, a flashlight with extra batteries, a small tool kit or at least an all-purpose tool, and a shovel and jumper cables (also handy if you want to jump someone).

Ya: Ya is not quite a full yes, but darn close. There is wiggle room as in, "Ya, but . . . ."

Town and City

Take a look at a Minnesota map and you can see that the name of some towns point directly to where settlers came from. There's a New Munich, New Prague, New London, New Sweden, New Ulm, New Germany, and a Finland. Many other place names were taken from Native American words that describe the area or that honor a specific person, usually a native with whom the white settlers had a good relationship, such as Sleepy Eye or Good Thunder. Some towns were given the first names of women settlers or the wives of dignitaries: Ada, Lydia, Isabella, Dorothy, Mabel, and Margie. There are plenty of towns that hold men's first names, too: Leo, Lyle, Hector, and Max. You can travel the world from Ceylon to Darfur to Geneva. Or you can find Independence, feel Welcome, or see the Sunrise.

Alexandria (9,647). This western Minnesota resort community has two sources for its name: the Egyptian city founded by Alexander the Great in 332 B.C.E., and Alexander Kinkead, one of the area's first settlers. Alexandria is the home of the Kensington Runestone, a large flat stone found by farmer Olaf Ohman in 1898 that was inscribed with runes similar to those used by 14th-century Norse people. If it's genuine, it would mean Scandinavian explorers were in North America in the 14th century; however, after being studied by linguistic experts, the consensus is that it's a hoax. Either way, you can find it at the downtown Runestone Museum.

Alpha (116). Bearing the name of the letter "A" in the Greek alphabet, Alpha shares its name with towns in Maryland, Indiana, and Illinois.

Alvarado (371). No one seems to know why a small town in northwestern Minnesota has the same name as a seaport and river in Mexico. It was first settled in 1879 and was originally called Snake, named for its location on the Snake River. When the Soo Line Railroad came through in 1903, its construction crew established the station name as Alvarado.

Apple Valley (49,983). In 1963 a builder named Orrin Thompson started building neighborhoods in Lebanon Township and he planted an apple tree in the yard of each home in some of his developments. By 1974, the township had become a statutory city named Apple Valley.

Artichoke (84). Minnesota doesn't have the climate to grow artichokes; this town's name was probably derived from a Dakota word that referred to the edible tuber roots of a species of sunflower. The tuber, called *pangi*, was abundant in the state.

Audubon (1,574). Famous ornithologist and artist John James Audubon's niece proposed the name for this town after she spent some

Did you know. . .

that since 1920, with the exception of metropolitan suburbs founded later on, no new place names have been added to the map of Minnesota?

TAKE5 BOYD HUPPERT'S FIVE
MINNESOTA "CAPITALS"

Boyd Huppert has worked for the Minneapolis-St. Paul NBC news affiliate, KARE-11, since 1996. He has won a national Emmy, numerous National Edward R. Murrow Awards and a National Headliner Grand Award for his feature reporting. Over the past few years he's traveled around Minnesota to collect gems for his special feature series, "Land of 10,000 Stories." Here are a few of his memories:

1. **Fountain: Sinkhole Capital of the World.** The Fountain area in southeastern Minnesota is home to more than 500 sinkholes. So proud is Fountain of its sinkholes the community has equipped one with a viewing platform. Yep, you can stand on a platform and look at a hole in the ground. No ticket required.

2. **Madison: Lutefisk Capital of the World.** Lutefisk, foisted upon Minnesota by its Scandinavian immigrants, translates to lye fish. (Lye is an essential ingredient in the creation of the gelatinous delicacy.) Jerry Osteraas has downed more than 8 pounds of Lutefisk in a single setting. He's been crowned Madison's lutefisk eating champion 17 times. It would have been 18, but for the contest's "retainage" rule. Contestants are required to keep the stuff down for one minute. No easy feat.

3. **Worthington: Turkey Capital of the World.** Folks in Worthington thought they had a lock on the turkey title until they found out Cuero, Texas, had also proclaimed itself Turkey Capital of the World. The two cities have agreed to settle their dispute with an annual turkey race — one heat in Worthington, the other in Cuero — to decide which city can rightfully call itself Turkey Capital the following year.

4. **Olivia: Corn Capital of the World.** Any town that puts a fiberglass cob on a 50-foot pedestal is serious about corn. Actually, Olivia would prefer if you didn't call it a cob. "You call it the ear of corn monument," I was once instructed by the Olivia Chamber of Commerce. Duly noted.

5. **Moose Lake: Agate Capital of the World.** Mix a few pails of Lake Superior agates into a large truck load of gravel. Gather several hundred people for a town festival. Then dump the mix an inch deep down Moose Lake's main drag. No scavenger hunt puts more noses in the gravel and butts in the air.

time camping with a group of tourists in the area in 1871. At the time, the town was going on its third name, Oak Lake. Before that it was called Windom and then Colfax. Four's a charm: the name Audubon has stuck. For now, anyway.

Ball Club (population unknown). The name of this railway village at the south end of Ball Club Lake on the Leech Lake Indian Reservation is translated from an Ojibwe name that means ball club (Native Americans in the area were fond of playing ball with a club or bat). The town was spelled as one word, Ballclub, until 1950.

TAKE 5 FIVE HAUNTED HAUNTINGS

1. **Forepaugh's Restaurant, St. Paul:** Diners may come in contact with the original owner, Joseph Forepaugh, and his lover, Molly, his maid. Both killed themselves, Forepaugh by gunshot and Molly by hanging. The ghost of Molly has been known to play tricks on employees and appear before guests at large parties held in the restaurant.

2. **Minneapolis City Hall:** John Moshik was supposedly the last man to be hanged in Minneapolis City Hall when he was put to death in 1898. His presence still haunts the fifth floor of the building, where he's been seen by custodians, lawyers, and judges.

3. **Billy's Bar & Grill, Anoka:** Patrons claim to see the ghosts of several young women who worked in the building when it was a brothel in the early 1900s.

4. **The Palmer House Hotel, Sauk Centre:** Guests at this hotel have experienced disembodied voices, thrown glasses in the bar, and a boy bouncing a ball down a hall. Sinclair Lewis once worked here, and some say his spirit still haunts the hotel.

5. **Blackwoods Bar & Grill, Two Harbors:** Though it was only built in 1994, plenty of patrons and employees have seen apparitions of females, heard footsteps behind them when no one is there, and felt cold breath on their necks.

Source: Minnesota Paranormal Study Group, www.minnesotaghosts.com

The Twin Cities

St. Paul and Minneapolis have been rivals for 150 years. In 1890, they kidnapped each other's census taker to prevent either city from claiming to have a larger population. When St. Paul completed the building of the Cathedral of Saint Paul, Minneapolis quickly followed suit with one of the most beautiful and ornate basilicas in the US. The cities were still going at it in the 1950s, both looking for a major league baseball team and both building stadiums in which to house them.

To out-of-staters, newcomers, and even Minnesotans outside of the Twin Cities, they are simply "The Cities," but each retains its own vibe and sensibility. Minneapolis razed many of its old buildings in the 1960s, giving over its skyline to sleek skyscrapers. St. Paul, on the other hand, preserved its architectural heritage and as a result has an older, more established feel.

Today, The Cities are the most populous urban area in the state and form part of the larger US Census division of Minneapolis-St. Paul-Bloomington, which is the country's 16th-largest metropolitan area and comprises 11 counties in Minnesota and two in Wisconsin. This area in turn is enveloped in the "combined statistical area" of Minneapolis-St. Paul-St. Cloud, which has a population of 3.5 million people, ranking it the 13th most populous such area in the US. Indeed, three in five Minnesotans live in the Greater Twin Cities area. And despite their longstanding rivalry, Minneapolitans and St. Paulites have combined to create one of the most livable urban environments in the country. In total, the Twin Cities have 136,900 acres of parks, lakes, ski areas, and golf courses, all within metro limits. Together, they host some of the best theater in the country, and are home to franchises in all four major professional sports. The Twin Cities have been named "one of the best places to do business in the US" by *MarketWatch*, and typically place near the top in liveability among U.S. metro areas. *Bloomberg Business Watch* ranked St. Paul and Minneapolis tenth and twelfth respectively in its survey of "America's 50 Best Cities" (Pittsburgh was number eleven, San Francisco number one, and Los Angeles number 50).

Walnut Grove

Although Walnut Grove may be the most famous town associated with Laura Ingalls Wilder, it was the only one she never specifically mentioned in her books. No matter. What Ingalls Wilder captured for readers — not just in America but around the world — was the frontier experience . . . the hardships, restlessness, the simple pleasures and decency.

Ingalls Wilder came to Walnut Grove from Big Woods in Wisconsin (they lived in a dugout in the creek until the house was built) when her father filed a preemption claim here. Although Walnut Grove was home to Ingalls Wilder from ages 7-12, it served as the setting for *Little House on the Prairie*. For a new generation brought up on television, *Little House* was their introduction to the frontier experience. Although the Ingalls family wanted to stay in Walnut Grove, Ingalls Wilder's father got a job on the railroad in Dakota Territory, and eventually the family settled in DeSmet, SD.

Wilder's own life was not an easy one. She married Almanzo Wilder, who later contracted diphtheria. She lost a son in childbirth. Financially, the homestead they would establish north of DeSmet was plagued by drought and fire. They moved to Spring Valley back in Minnesota before trying Florida and then Mansfield. It took 20 years of scraping by before the Wilders had a little scratch in their pocket.

With the publication of *Little House in the Big Woods* in 1931, the pioneering Wilder became a celebrated writer and wealthy beyond her wildest dreams. (*The Saturday Evening Post*, for example, paid her in excess of $30,000 for the serialization rights to her best-selling novel *Free Land*.)

She received the Newbery Honor Book award three times. When she died at the age of 90, she could not have known just how widely she succeeded in her humble motivation to make sure her memories, and through them the memories of the frontier, would be preserved and available for the children of today.

They said it

"None of the stores had signs, and I was informed that some stores had only been in business a few months and it was not time to expect them to get up signs; while the older ones were well-known to everybody, and where was the need of their having signs?"
— Clifton Johnson, *Highways and Byways of the Mississippi Valley*,
NY: Macmillan Co., 1906, referring to Dobbsdale, a village
in the southern part of the state

Bejou (93). The French greeting *bonjour* ("good day") is the source of the name of this town, which was host to fur traders and voyageurs in the 1800s. "Bejou" became a common Ojibwe salutation, much like the American greeting, "How do you do?"

Bird Island (1,195). A favorite camping place for Native Americans and trappers, Bird Island is so named because of its grove of large trees that was home to many wild birds. The grove was surrounded by sloughs, like an island.

Blue Earth (3,247). The Sisseton Dakota used a bluish-green pigment derived from a layer of shale found in the rock bluff of a nearby river. That river is also called Blue Earth.

Brooklyn Park (75,156). The sixth-largest city in Minnesota, Brooklyn Park was once Brooklyn Township (as was Brooklyn

Did you know. . .

that when 3M chose Maplewood as its headquarters, neighboring St. Paul tried to annex the land so that 3M would fall within its city limits? The people of Maplewood decided to form their city to keep 3M within its borders. Today, Maplewood remains the home of the Post-it Note.

Center), a location named by settlers from Brooklyn, MI. It became a city in 1969.

Carp. Carp is an unincorporated town (hence no population numbers) that was named after a fish that was nowhere near the site. A lumber camp cook gave the town its name after seeing sucker fish running up the Rapid River that were mistaken for carp.

Ceylon (372). In Asia, Ceylon is a large island adjoining India. The Minnesota town's name came from the boxes of Ceylon tea that lined the shelves in the local general store when the town was being established in 1900.

Climax and Fertile (264 and 839). Climax and Fertile are tiny towns in Polk County just 32 miles apart. Climax was founded in 1896 and was named after a chewing tobacco company whose motto was "Climax Plug Tobacco: The grand old chew." In 1996 the town held a contest and chose "Climax: More than just a feeling" as its motto. Fertile was named after Fertile, Iowa, where some of the town's first settlers came from. Legend has it that a local newspaper ran a headline after a car crash that read, "Fertile woman dies in Climax," but proof is lacking.

Darfur (137). The town of Darfur was named after the region in Sudan, but a common joke is that two Scandinavian railroad men came up with the name when they asked, "Why you stop dar fur?"

Did you know. . .

that there are 44 cities in Minnesota whose boundaries are in more than one county?

Duluth (86,211). Originally settled by the Sioux and Ojibwe (anglicized as Chippewa), the area was claimed for France in 1679 by Daniel Greysolon, Sieur du Lhut. Du Lhut was one of eight Frenchmen who made a canoe journey to Lake Superior in 1678 to explore the country farther west and attempt to ally with the Native Americans for fur trading. The city is built into a steep, rocky cliffside on the shores of Lake Superior.

Embarrass (691). This town got its name from a nearby river that bore the same name. The word "embarrass" comes from a French word that means to hinder, confuse or to be complicated, and that's how French trappers described the Embarrass River: it was too full of debris and obstacles for fur traders to use it to traverse the area.

Good Thunder (569). This railroad village was named after a Winnebago chief whose village was just east of the site. The chief was said to be a friend of the white people and in 1862 refused the overtures of the Dakota to join in the war against settlers. Good Thunder

TAKE5 FIVE MINNESOTA
BIG BUILDS

1. **The world's largest pelican** stands at the base of the Mill Pond dam on the Pelican River, right in downtown Pelican Rapids. The 15-1/2 feet tall concrete statue was built in 1957.

2. **The Minneapolis Sculpture Garden** is the largest urban sculpture garden in the country.

3. **The Guthrie Theater** is the largest regional playhouse in the US.

4. **The Grand Mound historic site**, the largest Indian burial mound in the upper Midwest, stands at the confluence of the Big Fork and Rainy Rivers on the Canadian border near International Falls.

5. **The world's largest Paul Bunyan Statue** resides in Akeley. The kneeling Paul Bunyan is 25 feet tall. He might be the claimed 33 feet tall, if he were standing, that is.

died several years later on the Missouri River, after his tribe had been forced to move into the Dakotas. Another story is that the name could have been for a Dakota scout who had converted to Christianity and who was also well-known by settlers in the area.

Independence (3,546). This Hennepin County town got its name from nearby Lake Independence, which took its name from a party of Fourth of July excursionists who wanted to honor the holiday.

International Falls (6,703). International Falls is located on the Canadian border at Koochiching Falls of the Rainy River. Rainy Lake and Rainy River were named for these falls, which once generated plentiful mists and falls before the water was used to generate power for the town's paper mills.

TAKE5 FIVE RAMSEY PLACES

Places named after Alexander Ramsey, the first territorial governor, the state's second governor, mayor of St. Paul, and US senator:

1. **Counties:** One in Minnesota, another in North Dakota.
2. **Cities:** One in Anoka County (a Twin Cities suburb), another in Illinois.
3. **Parks:** Alexander Ramsey Park, Redwood Falls (the largest municipal park in Minnesota); Ramsey Park, Stillwater.
4. **Schools:** Alexander Ramsey Elementary School, Montevideo; Ramsey International Fine Arts Center (formerly Alexander Ramsey Junior High School), Minneapolis; Alexander Ramsey Senior High School (merged with Frank B. Kellogg High School to become Roseville Area High School in 1986).
5. **Buildings:** Alexander Ramsey House, St. Paul; Ramsey Town Center, Ramsey MN.

Kanaranzi (286). This township was named after a nearby creek, which originally was spelled *Karanzi*, a Dakota word that meant "where the Kansas were killed."

Kettle River (168). The original town site was called Finland, but eventually took the name of the nearby river. The Finnish word *kattilajoki* means "kettle river city."

Mahnomen (1,200). This town gets its name from the Chippewa word for wild rice, a staple and sacred food of the Native Americans in Minnesota. Gambling has since supplanted rice as a staple here. Mahnomen is on the White Earth Reservation in northwestern Minnesota and is home to the Shooting Star Casino, which is owned and operated by the White Earth Reservation Tribal Council.

Menahga (1,220). *Menahga* is the Ojibwe word for the blueberry and is memorialized by Henry W. Longfellow in *The Song of Hiawatha*.

Minneapolis (407,207). Minnesota's largest city could have been named All Saints, Hennepin, Lowell, Brooklyn, or Albion, but in the end, Minneapolis won out. The name is a compound of the words Minnehaha and the Greek word *polis*, meaning "city". Minnehaha is the name of a creek and waterfall within the city. A Dakota word for waterfall is *haha*, and the word *minne* means "water."

Mizpah (78). *Mizpah* is the Hebrew word for "watchtower." It is used in the salutation, "The Lord watch between me and thee, when we are absent one from another." (Genesis 31:49).

Money Creek (547). This town got its name from the nearby Money Creek, where legend has it some traveler got his wallet and its contents wet in the creek and spread out the bank notes on a bush to dry. A gust of wind blew the money back into the water, and some of it was never recovered.

Montevideo (5,233). This Latin name means "from the mountain I see" or "mount of vision." Apparently its founders were delighted with the area's view overlooking the valleys of the Minnesota and Chippewa rivers. In 1905, the mayor of Montevideo, Uruguay, presented the Uruguayan flag to the town. The two towns have been sister cities for years. In 1949, Montevideo, Uruguay, gave the Minnesota town an 11-foot bronze statue of Jose Artigas, Uruguay's leader of independence. The statue is in the center of a plaza in downtown Montevideo, Minnesota. (Incidentally, it's pronounced mont-uh-vid-ee-oh.)

Nimrod (75). This tiny town in Wadena County is named for the grandson of Ham, called, in Genesis, "a mighty hunter before the Lord." He's reputed to have directed the construction of the Tower of Babel.

North Pole. This was the name of a proposed village just north of the city of Bemidji on the shore of Lake Bemidji. A post office was created in November 1940 as the county board had hopes of raising revenue with its postmark during the Christmas holiday. However, Gov. Joseph A. A. Burnquist said there was no valid reason to incorporate such a village, as there was no business except a summer resort hotel and a store. The name still appears on state highway maps.

Pipestone (9,395). Catlinite, the red pipestone found near here, has been quarried by Native Americans for hundreds of years. Longfellow referred to the stone and the legend of its first use to make the peace pipe in *Song of Hiawatha*: "From the red stone of the quarry / With his hand he broke a frag-

Did you know. . .

that Bloomington and Minneapolis are the farthest northern-latitude cities to host a World Series game?

ment, / Moulded it into a pipe-head, / Shaped and fashioned it with figures."

Rochester (111,402). Rochester was named after Rochester, NY, by George Head, who had lived in New York before coming to Minnesota in 1855. The rapids of the nearby Zumbro River reminded him of the Genesee River in New York. Rochester, MN, is best known as the home of the world-renowned Mayo Clinic.

Rollingstone (697). This town is named after the Rollingstone River whose Dakota name is *eyan-omen-man-met-pah*, which means "the stream where the stone rolls." Troops who came to the state in the early 1800s to build what is now Fort Snelling called the stream the Tumbling Rock.

TAKE5 COUNTY NAMES
AND WHAT THEY MEAN

The names of many Minnesota counties have been inspired by Indian terms: Kandiyohi County is from the Dakota language and means "where the buffalo fish come." Kanabec is the Ojibwe word for "snake." Here are some others:

1. **Chisago County.** The county's largest lake was named after *ki-chi-sago*, Ojibwe for "large and lovely." The original name was Chisaga, but a subsequent typographical error was never corrected.

2. **Koochiching County.** From *ouchichiq*, a Cree word adopted by the Ojibwe that means "neighbor lake and river," referring to Rainy Lake and Rainy River.

3. **Wadena County.** This name comes from a common Ojibwe word meaning "a little round hill." Wadena was the name of an old trading post in the area.

4. **Watonwan County**. From the Dakota word *watanwan*, meaning "fish bait" or "where fish bait abounds."

5. **Yellow Medicine County.** Named after the Yellow Medicine River, the name of which comes from the Dakota word *pajutazee*, which refers to the long, yellow grasses in the region.

They said it

Sebeka (710). Sebeka comes from the Ojibwe word *sibi* or *zibi*, meaning "the village or town beside the river."

Sleepy Eye (3,365). This town was named after Sleepy Eye, a chief of the Sisseton Dakota. Sleepy Eye signed the treaties of Prairie du Chien in 1825 and 1830, of St. Peter's in 1836, and Traverse des Sioux in 1851. Sleepy Eye's remains are buried under a monument in the town. It bears this inscription: "Ish-tak-ha-ba, Sleepy Eye, always a friend of the whites. Died 1860."

St. Cloud (65,986). To reflect the city's French heritage, St. Cloud was named after a suburb of Paris. Today St. Cloud is referred to as "Granite Country" because of the large deposits of granite that are mined and shipped all over the world.

St. Paul (297,640). Incorporated in 1854, St. Paul is the state capital and sits at the confluence of the Minnesota and Mississippi Rivers. The birthplace of F. Scott Fitzgerald, St. Paul is the home of the Science Museum of Minnesota, the Minnesota Wild hockey team, and *A Prairie Home Companion.*

Taopi (94). This town was named in honor of Taopi (Wounded Man), a leader of the farmer band of the Dakota, who died in March 1869. He was one of the first converts to Christianity at the Redwood mission on the Minnesota River and at the time of the Dakota War of 1862 was friendly to white settlers and aided in the rescue of many.

Viking (92). The Rev. Hans P. Hansen, a Norwegian Lutheran pastor, gave this township its name. Viking is often translated as "sea king," but more often means a member of medieval pirate crews of Norway who ravaged the coasts of western and southern Europe for centuries.

Warroad (1,700). Located near the Lake of the Woods, Warroad was once one of the largest Chippewa villages on the lake. The Chippewa fought a long war against the Sioux for the lake's rice fields. The Sioux, who were living on the prairies of the Red River Valley, would invade the territory by coming up the Red and Roseau rivers. This route ended at the mouth of the Warroad River. This was the old "war road."

Waubun (1,792). An Ojibwe name meaning "the east", "the morning" and "the twilight of dawn," it too is mentioned in Longfellow's *The Song of Hiawatha*, spelled "wabun" and meaning "the east wind." When the Soo Line Railroad was built through the county in 1903-04, the general manager and his chief engineer named the stations as they moved the line north. All towns on the reservation had to have native names.

Walnut Grove (599). This town was named for a 100-acre grove of black walnut trees on Plum Creek about a mile or two southwest of the town. The town is known as one of the stops on the Ingalls family's travels. It was home to author Laura Ingalls Wilder, whose father, Charles, was the town's first justice.

Winona (27,582). Winona, located in southeastern Minnesota, sits on a sandbar in the Mississippi Valley, surrounded by water and high bluffs. Winona honors its Dakota heritage through its name, which means "first-born daughter."

Weather

Minnesota is known for its harsh weather. An old joke involves a man who moves to Duluth and is asked by an out-of-stater what Minnesota is like in the summer. He answers, "I don't know—I've only lived here 13 months!" Actually, the story is a bit off: There is a summer, and it's a nice one; unfortunately, it's short and accompanied by mosquitoes.

Minnesota lies halfway between the North Pole and the equator, and polar air can sweep down through the state at any time, although it's most common during the winter, when temperatures can sink as low as -50° F. On the other hand, warm air from the Gulf of Mexico and the southwest US can flow up into the state, heating things up (114° F is the record) and keeping it hot for days. Moderate Pacific Ocean air currents brings with them mild temperatures and light precipitation. November of 2009 was amazingly warm, for example, due to warm winds hailing from the Pacific Northwest.

Minnesota has nothing if not four distinct seasons. Winter is dreaded, but also embraced; when the snow begins to fall and ice forms, kids of all ages rush to lace up skates for that first glide of the season. And when the winter pain ends, it feels so good: Every Minnesotan knows the exhilaration of that first 70-degree (or even 50-degree) spring day after a long winter. Summer is something to savor, whether lolling on a lakeside dock, or enjoying a meal outside on a warm Twin Cities evening. Fall comes early and is bittersweet: crisp and often clear, but

TAKE5 FIVE COLDEST US CITIES
YEAR-ROUND

Annual mean temperatures from 250 major weather stations in the continental US

1. **Mount Washington, New Hampshire:** 27.2° F
2. **International Falls, Minnesota:** 37.4° F
3. **Marquette, Michigan:** 38.7° F
4. **Duluth, Minnesota:** 39.1° F
5. **Caribou, Maine:** 39.2° F

Source: CurrentResults.com

holding the distinct possibility of a thunderstorm, or even a blizzard.

True, it's not like the olden days: central heating and air conditioning have blunted the worst effects of the weather, as has travel by car rather than horse. Still, spend a year in Minnesota, and you'll become well-acquainted with cold, heat, wet, wind, and all manner of other meteorological phenomena. Weather might not define the state and its people, but the elements are still a force to be reckoned with, and everyone has got a story or three to tell about a memorable tornado, blizzard, or flood. Ultimately, Minnesotans wear their unpredictable and sometimes severe weather like a badge of honor.

Did you know. . .

that rainwater from Target Field, home of the Minnesota Twins baseball team, is collected in tanks and used to hose down stadium seats and walkways?

Did you know. . .

that some northern Minnesotans believe that the higher a beaver builds his lodge, the more severe the coming winter will be?

TAKE5 FIVE LARGEST SNOWFALLS
IN THE TWIN CITIES

1. **28.4 inches:** Oct. 31-Nov. 3, 1991 (Halloween Blizzard)
2. **21.1 inches:** Nov. 29-Dec. 1, 1985
3. **20.0 inches:** Jan. 22-23, 1982
4. **17.4 inches:** Jan. 20-21, 1982
5. **16.8 inches:** Nov. 11-12, 1940

Source: Minnesota Climatology Working Group

AT A GLANCE

- Highest temperature on record: 114° F, Beardsley, July 29, 1917, and Moorhead, July 6, 1936
- Warmest month: July; 83.3° F daily maximum, 63° F daily minimum, 73.2° F monthly average (Minneapolis-St. Paul. Airport)
- Lowest temperature on record: -60° F, Tower, February 2, 1996
- Coldest month: January; 21.9° F daily maximum, 4.3° F daily minimum, 13.1° F monthly average (Minneapolis-St. Paul. Airport)
- Annual average rainfall: 29.4 inches (Minneapolis-St. Paul. Airport)
- Most extreme 24-hour temperature change: 71° F, Lamberton, April 3, 1982
- Least cloud cover: June to August
- Most cloud cover: November and December

They said it

"Ball lightning is a rare, mysterious glowing blob associated with thunderstorms under the right conditions. The National Weather Service cited one report in a house near St. Cloud on June 8, 1973. It was described as 'dancing around . . . leaving bullet-sized holes in walls and larger holes in ceilings.'"

— **Ask a Climatologist, Minnesota Department of Natural Resources**

All Hail King Boreas!

When you have a famously long and severe winter, what to do? Well, you can either bemoan your miserable fate, or turn winter into a cause for celebration.

In 1886, booming St. Paul staged its first winter carnival, a festival that included skiing, snow shoeing, tobogganing, and a large ice castle.

There was also "a blanket toss," an event based on an ancient practice of northern Native peoples in which a blanket is held by a group and used to propel an individual as high as 35 feet in the air. The technique was employed to scan the tundra for game, or detect predators or other threats. The St. Paul Bouncing Team continues the carnival tradition to this day.

The carnival's most spectacular element is the ice palace. These elaborate, luminous, magical works of art and engineering are guaranteed to turn even the sternest winter scrooge into an awestruck fan of the colder months. Because their construction requires so much time and money, ice palaces are constructed only every few years.

The Winter Carnival was established to dispel East Coast perceptions that St. Paul is a frigid, prairie wasteland. It is now the nation's oldest and largest winter festival, hosting more than 75 events which are attended by more than 350,000 people. The Carnival generates roughly five million dollars in economic activity for the region.

The carnival's signature event is the parade, during which Vulcanus Rex ceremoniously brings his fire down on King Boreas. This tradition is part of an elaborate carnival mythology starring King Boreas, the "King of the Winds." According to legend, King Boreas came upon the beautiful city of St. Paul while traveling and proclaimed the magical spot "the winter playground of the Realm of Boreas." For 10 days, Boreas, his Prime Minister and the Queen of Snows lord over a festival packed with winter activities, as well as coronations, proclamations, dances, feasts, and the like. Fellow travelers include the King's Royal Guard, Senior King Winter, the Queen of the Northlands, Junior King Frost, the Queen of the Snowflakes, Klondike Kate, and numerous attendants and hangers-on.

But the party can't last forever, and there is a villain lurking. Vulcanus Rex, the god of Fire, wishes to stomp out Boreas's chilly festivities and put an end to the winter fun. Rex crashes the King's ice castle and confronts the Royal Guard, forcing Boreas into exile among the gods, to return only the following winter. Rex doesn't work alone; he is accompanied by the Vulcan Krewe, a devilish force attired in red running suits, complete with capes, goggles and headgear. The Krewe arrives in a vintage fire truck, and some carnival attendees are "knighted" or "marked" by this fiery band of poor sports.

Each year, a new King Boreas and his royal family are nominated and crowned. Similarly, the Order of Fire and Brimstone, a fraternal club, selects the Vulcan Krewe for the following year, including a new Vulcanus Rex.

Boreas and other cold weather royals (as well as the villainous Vulcanus Rex and Crewe) make hundreds of appearances throughout the year, promoting volunteerism and other causes. The various carnival offices, costumes, rituals, and traditions are, of course, a lot of fun, but they have also provided a novel way to strengthen community engagement and extend philanthropy.

AVERAGE SEASONAL TEMPERATURES REGIONALLY

	North	South
Spring	36°F	44°F
Summer	60°F	70°F
Fall	38°F	46°F
Winter	6°F	16°F

The Many Climates Of Minnesota

Minnesota has fertile farmlands that include portions of the US Corn Belt in the south, while sub-arctic forest stretches across the northern region of the state. The Great Lakes storm belt touches the eastern portion of Minnesota and the Great Plains begin in the western portion of the state. July's daily highs reach 85°F in the south, and 70°F along the northern shore of Lake Superior. The average daily high temperatures in January hits 15°F in the northern part of the state and 25°F in southern Minnesota. Despite these variations, the state is cold enough throughout that in an average winter, most of Minnesota will have continuous snow cover from the middle of December to the middle of March.

Minnesota really has several climates instead of one monolithic climate; witness the weather surrounding Lake Superior, which cools neighboring land in summer and keeps it (relatively) warm in the winter. Water's effects are also felt on the southern banks of the Mississippi and Minnesota rivers, which trap solar heat and warm the surrounding area, while water vapor from the river will prevent an area from cooling down overnight, making for warm evenings.

On the other hand, Tower, located in the northeastern part of the state, is so cold in part because it sits on bedrock with a thin layer of soil that doesn't retain much solar heat. And the rolling land means cold, dense air can pool at night. Finally, urban weather is different than rural weather: In cities, winters are warmer and spring tends to arrive earlier.

THAT'S BRISK

Minnesota winters can be bitterly cold with wind chills making the frigid temperatures feel that much icier. Minnesota's coldest town is Embarrass, which is bordered by the Vermilion Range to the north and the Laurentian Divide to the south. Moraines (boulders and debris from glaciers) hit the valley at right angles. These natural features push cold air down, where it collects at night. During the winter of 1996-97, Embarrass saw six nights colder than -50°F.

SNOW

Snowfall is predictably unpredictable. It has arrived as early as September and been on the ground as late as May, and it's not unusual to see 4 inches fall at one time any time from mid-November to mid-April. The Halloween Blizzard of 1991, when 8 inches fell, was the earliest the state has accumulated more than 6 inches in one day. And on April 29, 1984, there was a little 7-inch dusting, the latest date for an accumulation of more than 6 inches. Snow has fallen in Minnesota in every month of the year except for July.

- Most snow in 24 hours: 36 inches, near Finland on Jan. 7, 1994
- Maximum single-storm snowfall: 46.5 inches, near Finland, Jan. 6-8, 1994
- Maximum seasonal snowfall: 170.5 inches, near Grand Portage, 1949-50
- Earliest measurable snowfall: 0.3 inches, International Falls, Sept. 14, 1964
- Latest measurable snowfall: 1.5 inches, Mizpah, June 4, 1935
- Maximum freeze depth: 3-4 feet in the south; 5-6 feet in the north

Did you know. . .

that Duluth recorded traces of snow on Aug. 31, 1949?

SNOW IN THE TWIN CITIES

- Annual average snowfall: 56.3 inches
- Average date of the first inch of snowfall: Nov. 18

TAKE5 FIVE MAJOR WEATHER EVENTS
OF THE TWENTIETH CENTURY

Minnesotans are fond of drawing up lists of worst weather events, be it the worst month for tornado outbreaks, most severe heat waves, most destructive blizzards, or worst floods in the recorded history of the state. Here is the Minnesota State Climatology Office's list of the worst events of the 1900s.

1. **1930s Dust Bowl.** The drought of the 1920s and 1930s is often ranked as the worst weather-related event in Minnesota. Two decades of dry, hot weather turned farm fields to dust, essentially creating deserts. Strong winds kicked up dust storms that lasted for months. The drought peaked in 1936.

2. **Armistice Day Blizzard.** In 1940, between Nov. 11th and Nov. 12th, more than 16 inches of snow fell on the Twin Cities, with 27 inches accumulating near St. Cloud. Twenty-foot drifts were reported near Willmar. The mild weather had lured many people outside, some of whom were then caught in the ensuing rain that quickly turned into snow, which soon became a blizzard. Winds gusted to 60 miles per hour and the temperature dropped by 40 degrees. The storm claimed the lives of 49 people, many of them hunters.

3. **1965 Floods and Tornadoes.** March of 1965 was too cold to melt river ice and spring landed suddenly in April, bringing with it rain and warm temperatures. The snow melted quickly, rivers weren't clear of ice, and the Mississippi, Minnesota, and St. Croix rivers overflowed.

- Average date of the first 2-inch snowfall: Nov. 29
- Average date of the first 4-inch snowfall: Dec. 20
- Average date of the last inch of snow cover: April 2

Source: National Weather Service

Teenagers, college students and prison inmates were put to work piling sandbags along river banks, and explosives were used to break up ice sheets, but the water still reached record levels. The next month, on May 5th and 6th, 12 tornadoes twisted through the state, with six meeting the ground close to the Twin Cities metro area. Fourteen people were killed during the outbreak. Some people reckon this as the worst Twin Cities weather event ever.

4. **1991 Halloween Blizzard.** This blizzard dropped more than 28 inches of snow on the Twin Cities, setting a record for the metro area. Duluth had the largest single storm total in history, with nearly 37 inches. School was canceled the next day, allowing kids around the state to play in the snow and gorge on Halloween treats.

5. **1997 Red River Flood.** The winter of 1996-97 brought record snowfall to the western edge of Minnesota and the Dakotas. In mid-April, the snow began to melt and the Red River and upper part of the Minnesota River rose and rose, reaching 26 feet above levels deemed hazardous. Water flooded over dikes and reached two miles inland in Grand Forks, ND, and East Grand Forks, MN.

Source: Minnesota State Climatology Office, Department of Natural Resources

"In Minnesota, the 10 o'clock news is just window-dressing for the
10 o'clock weather."

— **Howard Mohr, author of *How to Talk Minnesotan*.**

WINTER STORMS AND BLIZZARDS

A snowfall is classified as a storm when 6 or more inches fall in 12
hours, or 8 inches fall within 24 hours. These events are typically
accompanied by freezing rain or sleet, strong winds, and cold temperatures. The state gets three to four winter storms a year. One of
the worst winter storms on record occurred in mid-January 1888 and
killed 200 people.

A blizzard technically refers to winds of 35 miles per hour or higher,
snow, blowing snow for three or more hours, visibility of a quarter mile
at most, and falling temperatures. These conditions have to last for
three or more hours for the storm to qualify as a blizzard. Minnesotans
see about two heavy snowfalls with blizzard conditions every year.

HALLOWEEN BLIZZARD

The Halloween Blizzard ran from Oct. 30 to Nov. 3, 1991, making
it one of the largest and longest blizzards in state history. The power
went out and stayed out for a week in some places and the National
Guard was called on to supply portable generators to some farms. In
the Twin Cities, 28.4 inches of snow fell, while Duluth got 37 inches
of the white stuff.

Did you know. . .

that after the devastating drought of 1976, the state, feeling
pressure from farmers and academia, set up a faculty position in
University of Minnesota's Department of Soil, Water and Climate
to help predict future disasters?

They said it

"It was cold out there, bitter, biting, cutting, piercing, hyperborean, marmoreal cold, and there were all these Minnesotans running around outdoors, happy as lambs in the spring."
— **Charles Kuralt, journalist known for his "On the Road" segments on the *CBS Evening News with Walter Cronkite*.**

Halloween in Minnesota is typically a chilly affair, but the 1991 blizzard turned witches, ghosts, and Teenage Mutant Ninja Turtles into cold-weather warriors who braved snow drifts and driving winds for their Mars bars. Most kids couldn't get further than a block or so, but if they ventured outside at all they were richly rewarded for their valiant efforts. Sleds, more commonly associated with Christmas vacation than Halloween, were hauled out from the garage and pressed into service to haul pint-sized monsters and princesses around on their rounds.

Blizzards are not exactly rare events in Minnesota, but this one arrived early in the season and came on very fast. A low pressure system moving up from Texas hit Southern Iowa on Oct. 30, and then on Halloween morning struck Minnesota and Wisconsin with a cocktail of wind, snow, sleet, and rain. By afternoon, heavy snow was falling and most of the state immobile. More than 20 people died as a result of the storm, mostly from heart attacks and shoveling snow.

- 30 to 50 mph, gusts of 60 mph
- Number of counties declared federal disaster areas: 11
- Total damage in dollars: $11.7 million
- Estimated number of people without power: 20,000
- Major roads closed: 180 miles of Interstate 90 from the South Dakota border to Rochester

Source: National Weather Service, Minnesota Department of Natural Resources

WHITE CHRISTMAS

Northern Minnesota is the most likely part of the state to have at least an inch of snow (or more) on Christmas Day. The far southwest part of the state has only a 60% chance of a white Christmas, while the odds in the Twin Cities are 72 percent. In 2009, the Twin Cities experienced a Christmas storm that dropped 7.2 inches of snow on the area, the third-biggest Christmas snowfall ever (1945 tops the list with 11.3 inches).

TAKE5 PETE BOULAY'S FIVE EARLY
WEATHER MEMORIES

Pete Boulay is the assistant state climatologist for the Department of Natural Resource's State Climatology Office. As a child growing up in Maplewood, a St. Paul suburb, Boulay eagerly awaited the first thunderstorm of the spring and the first snowflakes in the fall. He went on to become a meteorologist, and now combines weather with history in his work as a climatologist.

1. **The snowstorms of Jan. 20-21, (17.4 inches), and Jan. 22-23, 1982 (20 inches).** The forecast for the first storm was for 1-3 inches of snow. By the next day, there was a snowfall total of 17.4 inches, a new record for the Twin Cities that was broken two days later. The second storm was the only occasion I can remember school being canceled at noon, and it had some of the most intense snowfall I have ever witnessed: Visibility was briefly down to a few yards, with vivid lightning and thunder.

2. **Cold outbreak of Dec. 17-25, 1983.** I saw -31°F on my indoor-outdoor thermometer and the Twin Cities International Airport had a minimum of -29°F on Dec. 19. More impressive were the cold "high" temperatures. The maximum temperature was -17°F on December 23. One strange thing I remember about the extreme cold was what happened when someone would open an outside door: A thick cloud of vapor would instantly form when the warm house air hit the bitterly cold air outside.

Did you know...

That the winter of 2013-14 represented the coldest such season in the Twin Cities in 35 years, and was one of the ten coldest on record?

3. **Snow of Sept. 24, 1985.** Measurable snow in September is very rare in the Twin Cities: It has only happened three times in 120 years. What made this .4 inches of September snowfall even more unusual is that it happened in the afternoon. It was enough to coat the ground and surprised a lot of people.

4. **73°F on March 7, 1987**. Kids were wearing shorts that day as the temperature reached the low 70s. The ground had thawed enough by then to bury a time capsule, which I intended to open 20 years later. In 2007, when I dug the capsule up, most of the items were ruined by water that had seeped into the 5-gallon bucket.

5. **105°F at Minneapolis-St. Paul on July 31, 1988**. It was the warmest day of the 1988 drought, with the highest recorded daytime temperature in the Twin Cities since the Dust Bowl era. Despite the temperature, it didn't feel as hot as it might have because the air was so dry and it was very windy. I positioned a mercury thermometer in the shade to record the temperature, but the wind blew my thermometer over and broke it.

AVERAGE NUMBER OF DAYS WITH A SNOW DEPTH OF. . .

- 1 inch: 100
- 3 inches: 79
- 6 inches: 54
- 9 inches: 34
- 12 inches: 24

TAKE5 FIVE SEVERE
TORNADOES

1. **Aug.21, 1883, Rochester.** 37 people were killed and 200 injured. The care provided to the injured led to the establishment of the Mayo Clinic.

2. **April 14, 1886, St. Cloud and Sauk Rapids.** A tornado lay waste to Sauk Rapids' main street, including the railroad office, two churches, a school, post office, flour mill, and court house. It also tossed 15 rail cars off the tracks. It was the deadliest of all tornadoes on record: A bride and groom and nine of their wedding party were among the 72 killed. The injury count was 213.

3. **June 22, 1919, Fergus.** Fergus falls victim to a tornado, which killed 59. The previous August, 36 people had been killed by a tornado at Tyler.

4. **June 16, 1992, Chandler.** The southwestern town was hit hard by Minnesota's biggest tornado outbreak. Twenty-two tornadoes were reported between 4 and 9 p.m. in 11 counties, the largest traveling at more than 260 mph. The outbreak killed one person, injured more than 40, and destroyed 40 homes and damages another 47.

5. **March 29, 1998, St. Peter.** The small southern town of St. Peter, home to Gustavus Adolphus College, was hit by a 1.25-mile-wide F3 twister which tore through in under a minute at speeds of up to 206 mph. A 6-year-old boy was killed; hundreds of homes were ripped from their foundations, roofs torn off, and windows blown out. Total damage to the area was $50 million. The only saving grace was that college students were on spring break and the campus nearly deserted.

They said it

I've been waiting for you to come back
Since you left Minneapolis
Snow covers the streetlamps and the windowsills
The buildings and the brittle crooked trees
Dead leaves of December
Thin skinned and splintered
Never gotten used to this bitter winter

**— Lucinda Williams, excerpt from the song "Minneapolis"
from the 2003 album *World Without Tears*. Williams is married
to producer and former Best Buy exec Tom Overby**

PRECIPITATION

The southeast part of the state gets approximately 34 inches of rain on average every year, while the northwest sees 19 or so inches.

- Maximum 24-hour total rain: 15.1 inches, Aug. 19, 2007, Hokah
- Maximum monthly total: 23.9 inches, Aug. 2007, Hokah
- Maximum annual total: 53.5 inches, 1991, St. Francis
- Minimum annual total: 6.4 inches, 1976, Ortonville

Sources: Minnesota Department of Natural Resources; Minnesota State Climatology Office, University of Minnesota

FLOODS

Snow melts quickly in the spring, often before iced-over rivers have broken up. Rain can also be heavy in the spring season, and this combination of rain and melting snow and ice is a recipe for flooding. In 1826, these conditions led to a 20-foot rise in the Mississippi's water level, sweeping away all low-lying buildings on the river bank.

The region that tends to see the most flooding in the state is the Red River Valley in northwestern Minnesota and eastern North Dakota. On April 26, 1997 flood waters crested at 66 inches in Pembina. This was part of a regional deluge as North Dakota and southern Manitoba also experienced major flooding when the Red River (which forms the border between North Dakota and Minnesota) overflowed its banks. The Minnesota communities most seriously affected were East Grand Forks, Moorhead, and Breckenridge.

Flash floods—when six or more inches of rain falls within 24 hours—usually happen in summer. The biggest flash flood in Minnesota's history was in July, 1972, when some locales received 15 inches of rain and major highways were closed for 16 days. In June 2012, flooding caused $100 million damage in Duluth and northeast Minnesota.

DROUGHT

The southwest and west central parts of the state are likely to experience severe drought once every 10 years. In eastern parts, it's once every 25 years, and once every 50 years in the northeast. The longest period without rain in the state: 79 days recorded at Beardsley, Canby, Marshall, and Dawson from Nov. 9, 1943, to Jan. 26, 1944.

THUNDERSTORMS

Thunderstorms have dumped so much rain on Minnesota that they've washed out roads and bridges, flooded homes, and swept away newly sown crops. Thunderstorms are most common from May to July. Southern Minnesota gets approximately 45 days of thunderstorms every year; that number drops to 30 days in the north.

TORNADOES

Minnesota is located on the northern edge of Tornado Alley (Texas, Oklahoma, Kansas, Missouri, East Nebraska, and West Iowa) and experiences about 25 tornadoes yearly. Tornadoes usually hit during spring and early summer between 4 and 8 p.m. Tornado activity increases when warm gulf air reaches the drier, cooler air common during Minnesota springs and summers. Although it would appear that there are more tornadoes now than in years past, meteorologists point out that this may be more of a statistical phenomenon than a real one: Doppler radar and spotter networks have made for more accurate numbers.

Tornadoes in Minnesota are generally on the ground for less than 5 miles and can be as narrow as 50 yards or more stretch more than a mile wide. At least seven really severe tornadoes (F5s, which reach speeds of 318 mph) have touched down in the state, with Freeborn, Polk, and Stearns counties seeing the most of such dangerous tornado activity. Since 1950, Minnesota has seen some 1,500 tornadoes injuring nearly 2,000 people and killing close to 100.

HEAT

Despite the long, cold winters, Minnesota summers can be scorchers: Temperatures in the Twin Cities have risen to 100°F, and hit 104°F in September 1931 at the State Fair. Keep in mind if it's humid, it can feel up to 15 degrees warmer. According to the state Department of Public Safety, at least 15 Minnesotans have died from extreme heat since 1993. Still, the heat doesn't tend to stick around for long. More than four consecutive days of extreme heat are rare, although in July 1936, Beardsley residents experienced 13 straight days of 100°F or more. A more recent heat wave was in late August and early September 2013 when there was a prolonged string of 90°+ temperature days in the Twin Cities. In dry regions of Minnesota, the spring can be just as hot as the summer, and Montevideo reached 88°F in March 1910.

They said it

"During the spring of 1965, Minnesota reeled under a succession of blizzards, floods, and tornadoes. Through it all the state Legislature debated daylight saving time with great fervor. Residents took it all, in stride, quipping that a Minnesotan was someone with snow in his yard and water in the basement of his roofless house, who did not know what time it was."

— **William E. Lass** from *Minnesota: A History*
(W.W. Norton & Co., New York: 1983)

The Natural World

The oldest rocks in Minnesota date back 3.6 billion years—almost as old as the earth itself — and you can see the outcrops of them at Granite Falls. Later tectonic activity created mile-high, iron-rich mountain ranges that eroded, becoming the Iron Range. Volcanoes erupted, spewing lava that cooled into rocks. Earthquakes created a rift valley from Lake Superior to Kansas. Warm water in the rift carried silica into volcanic rock, creating agate, the state rock.

Two million years ago, once tectonic plates, volcanoes and earthquakes had had their say, the Ice Age began. Glaciers ground their way through the region, scraping and sculpting the land and leaving distinct features, along with sand, gravel, and rock, in their wake. The rolling hills of Minnesota are glacial vestiges. The glacier from the Kansan Ice Age—roughly 400,000 years ago—scooped up limestone on its travels over the continent, depositing it in parts of Minnesota.

The most recent glacial ice advanced into Minnesota 12,000 to 10,500 years ago. It was glaciers that deposited aggregates while glacial till formed the parent soil for the state's farmlands and glacial lakes would form to define the Minnesota landscape.

In many ways, geography and geology have defined Minnesota. They have in large part provided the economic impetus for its development, defined its identity, and nurtured its soul.

STATE SYMBOLS
- Flower: Pink and White Lady's Slipper
- Tree: Red or Norway pine (*Pinus resinosa*)
- Bird: Common loon (*Gavia immer*)
- Fish: Walleye (*Stizostedion vitreum*)
- Fruit: Honeycrisp apple
- Gem: Lake Superior agate
- Butterfly: Monarch
- Grain: Wild rice (*Zizania aquatica* or *Zizania palustris*)
- State mushroom: Morel (*Morchella esculenta*)

LATITUDES
- Longitude: 89° 34'W to 97° 12'W
- Latitude: 43° 34'N to 49° 23'N

The geographic center of the Gopher State is in Crow Wing County, 10 miles southwest of Brainerd, at longitude 95° 19.6'W and latitude 46° 1.5'N. The capital, St. Paul, is at longitude 93°5.4'W and latitude 44°56.4'N. Other cities at nearly the same latitude: Simferopol, Crimea; Bordeaux, France; and Turin, Italy.

Did you know. . .

that Cabela's, a chain devoted to fishing, hunting, and outdoor gear, ranks among the state's leading tourist attractions? There are four Minnesota locations: East Grand Forks, Woodbury, Rogers and Owatonna. The latter two are true mega-stores, boasting a combined 315,000 square feet of floor space, and each featuring a restaurant, fudge shop, aquarium, extensive taxidermy displays, and outdoor kennel for dogs to enjoy while their owners shop.

TAKE5 FIVE LARGEST LAKES
IN MINNESOTA BORDERS

1. **Red Lake (both "Upper" and "Lower"):** 288,800 acres
2. **Mille Lacs Lake:** 132,516 acres
3. **Leech Lake:** 111,527 acres
4. **Lake Winnibigoshish:** 58,544 acres
5. **Lake Vermilion:** 40,557 acres

Source: Minnesota Department of Natural Resources

AS THE CROW FLIES
- Land area: 83,574 square miles (12th largest in the nation. Michigan and Utah are 11th and 13th, respectively.)
- East-west distance: 360 miles
- North-south distance: 407 miles

HIGHS AND LOWS
- Highest point: Eagle Mountain (Cook County), 2,301 feet
- Lowest point: surface of Lake Superior, 602 feet above sea level
- Mean elevation: 1,200 feet

DISTANCE FROM MINNEAPOLIS TO MAJOR CENTERS
- Atlanta: 703 miles
- Chicago: 253
- Dallas: 615
- Detroit: 431
- Denver: 571
- Los Angeles: 1,204
- Miami: 1,114
- New Orleans: 807
- New York: 762
- Phoenix: 1,047
- San Francisco: 1,278

TAKE 5 BRYAN WOOD'S NATURAL
MINNESOTA WONDERS

Bryan Wood is co-executive director of the Audubon Center of the North Woods, a residential environmental learning center in Sandstone, Minnestoa. He oversees land management, and is the instructor for the center's college courses and Elderhostel programs.

1. **Canoe Country.** Minnesota is the land of 10,000 lakes, but in actuality there are more than 15,000 lakes, 10 acres or larger. Nowhere can that be experienced more fully than in northeastern Minnesota, in the Boundary Waters Canoe Area Wilderness, and Voyageurs National Park. With a combined 1.6 million acres of federally protected land and water, you can paddle and hike through an area where you can see wolves, moose, black bear, loons, and bald eagles.

2. **Mississippi River Valley.** When the glaciers descended upon Minnesota from 100,000 until just 10,000 years ago, they covered nearly all parts of the state under as much as 2 miles of ice, flattening hills and scraping away soil. The southeastern corner of Minnesota is known as the "Driftless Area," where the glaciers never reached, leaving rolling hills reminiscent of the Appalachians. When the glaciers melted, they drained through the Minnesota, St. Croix, and Mississippi rivers and converged in southeastern Minnesota to carve out the great Mississippi River Valley. Over a mile wide, the valley is marked by 300 to 400 bluffs, and the river is dotted with islands and backwaters to explore.

3. **Minnesota's North Shore of Lake Superior.** Nearly 400 million years ago, the continent threatened to split in half through the Mid-Continental Rift. This pulling apart of land caused magma to spew up and harden into basalt and rhyolite. After the weight of this rock

collapsed upon itself, it created a deep basin that would eventually be filled in from the melting of the last glacier 10,000 years ago. Minnesota's North Shore has National Scenic Highway 61, Superior National Forest, seven state parks, the Superior Hiking Trail, and the Gitchi-Gami State Trail. All this is along the largest body of freshwater in the world.

4. **Three Biomes.** Minnesota is unique in that it has three major terrestrial biomes within its borders. Tallgrass Prairie reaching 10 feet tall historically covered the western edge of the state and pockets can still be found in areas like Blue Mounds State Park and Big Stone National Wildlife Refuge. The Eastern Broadleaf Forest extended from the Atlantic Ocean all the way over through central and west-central Minnesota. This forest is characterized by oak, maple, basswood, elm, walnut, and cherry trees, and the amazing spring wildflowers that cover the forest floor every May. The Boreal Forest covers the north-central and northeastern part of the state and is comprised of pines, fir, spruces, birch, and aspen.

5. **Three Watersheds.** No other state can claim to have three major watersheds within its borders. Depending on where you are, a drop of water could trickle down a rock and end up in the Gulf of Mexico through the Mississippi Watershed. Or it could flow out to the Atlantic Ocean through the St. Lawrence Seaway. Or it could make its way up to the Arctic Ocean through the Hudson Bay Watershed.

They said it

WATER, WATER EVERYWHERE

Minnesota ranks eighth among states for having the most water within its borders. The waters of Minnesota flow north to Hudson Bay, east to the Atlantic, and south to the Gulf of Mexico. The Mississippi River, the longest and largest river in North America, begins at Lake Itasca in northern Minnesota.

- Water area: 7,326 square miles
- Number of lakes larger than 10 acres: 11,842
- Number of rivers and streams: 6,564 (Collectively, 92,000 miles long. In fact, if you count wetlands, more than 13 million acres are covered by water.)
- Deepest inland lake: Portsmouth Mine Pit, 450 feet and rising
- Deepest natural lake: Lake Saganaga, 240 feet
- Longest shoreline: Lake Vermilion, 290 miles
- State-managed water trails: 31
- Recreational watercraft per capita: One boat for every six residents. (Minnesota is ranked first in the nation.)
- Miles of canoeing routes: 4,257
- Number of managed water trails: 31
- Number of public lake accesses: 3,000+

Source: Minnesota Department of Natural Resources

Walleye

Fishing to Minnesotans is simply a birthright. In the 24 hours before the inland season opens, more than 35,000 anglers (30 per minute) will purchase a fishing license. In total, 1.2 million Minnesotans will buy an angling license in any given year; that is one in every five Minnesotans, making the state the runaway leader in the number of fishing licenses sold per capita.

And the unquestionable king of the Minnesota fishery is the walleye, so named because of those eyes—cat eyes that reflect light. The walleye is not prized for its eyes, however, but rather for its great tasting, white, flaky flesh. The inimitable taste of a shore lunch is a memory that is burned into the minds of Minnesotans at a young age.

Minnesotans harvest some 3.5 million walleye every year, totalling 35 million pounds. Two towns, Garrison and Baudette, claim the title of Walleye Capital of the World. Every serious Minnesota angler still knows the name Leroy Chiovitte and the size of the record walleye (17 pounds, 8 ounces) he landed more than 30 years ago at the mouth of the Seagull River at Lake Saganaga. As early as 1965, Minnesota gave the walleye the exalted status of state fish.

The Land of 10,000 Lakes has 1,200 of them with fishable walleye populations. The Minnesota Department of Natural Resources stocks more than 350 lakes with 167,579 pounds of fingerlings and another 200-plus lakes with 261 million fry. It also stocks lakes with 50,000 walleye yearlings and 30,000 adults.

Sports fishing in Minnesota is a $1.58 billion industry. Sports fishing accounts for more than 102 million pounds of harvest each year, while commercial fishing accounts for only 4.5 million pounds. The pursuit of the walleye is such that it has created a whole host of sub-industries like the sale of minnows. There are now, for example, more than 830 minnow retailers and 283 minnow dealers in the state.

Fishing to Minnesotans is more than an industry, it is a tangible connection to nature and to forefathers. The simple pleasures of hooking a walleye and consuming it a few hours later is a pleasure that harkens back to the satisfaction our ancestors must have felt across the millennium.

TAKE5 MINNESOTA'S FIVE
LONGEST RIVERS

1. **Mississippi River:** 681.3 miles (in Minnesota)
2. **Red River:** 457.1 miles
3. **Minnesota River:** 370.6 miles
4. **Rainy River:** 292.1 miles
5. **Bigfork River:** 220.7 miles

Source: Minnesota Department of Natural Resources

BIRDS AND ANIMALS

- Mammal species in Minnesota: 78
- Amphibian species in Minnesota: 22
- Reptile species in Minnesota: 29
- Bird species in Minnesota: 428
- Bird species that are year-round residents: 44
- Timberwolves: 2,900+
- White-tailed deer: 1.5 million
- Black bears: 20,000-30,000
- Moose: 7,500

HUNTING

(Numbers taken annually)
- Deer: 158,854

Did you know...

that Minnesota boasts 90,000 miles of lake and river shoreline, more shoreline than California, Florida, and Hawaii combined?

Did you know...

that of Minnesota's 87 counties, only four (Mower, Olmsted, Pipestone, Rock) have no natural lakes?

- Bear: 4,110
- Moose: 125
- Coyote: 14,000
- Pheasant: 358,000
- Wild turkey: 8200

BUZZZZZZZ

Although the loon is the state bird of Minnesota, many Minnesotans — only half in jest — say that honor should belong to the mighty mosquito. So ubiquitous in the minds of Minnesotans is the mosquito that many people say there are really only two seasons in Minnesota: winter and mosquito season.

Minnesota's ferocious mosquitoes (and their bloodthirsty relatives: the black fly, deer fly, horse fly, stable fly and midge) have been immortalized in legend, song, and on T-shirts. The little beasts — females only, of course — have been known to drive huge moose out of the woods at a frenzied gallop to escape their relentless attacks.

The Minnesota mosquito is nothing if not resilient. In total, there are 50 species of mosquitoes in Minnesota, and at least 28 of those like the taste of human blood. A single female bite contributes directly to 100 eggs. Although a typical adult life cycle is only two to four weeks, a fine hunting mosquito can bite up to three times during that period.

Although the Minnesota mosquito measures on average just under a half-inch, it has been responsible for creating a whole industry dedicated to its extermination. Indeed, even the government has 18 elected county commissioners on a board called the Metropolitan Mosquito Control District to plot strategies to keep the tiny mosquito at bay.

It is the subject not only of campfire discussions, but also debate in the Legislature. The Minnesota mosquito is perhaps the most democratic of species, as likely to attack a captain of industry or a government official as it is a fisherman about to make his first cast.

They said it

ENDANGERED PLANTS AND ANIMALS
- Federally endangered and threatened: 9
- State endangered and threatened: 197
- State special concern: 242

FORESTS
Minnesota's forests at one time covered more than two-thirds of the state. Although they have been greatly reduced, the state has planted nearly 5 million trees and more than 30,000 acres have been reforested through natural processes, seeding, and planting.
- Forested area: 16.3 million acres (covers 29% of the state)
- Rank among states for most area covered by forests: 17
- Number of private individuals who own timberland in Minnesota: 103,300
- Forest ownership accounted for by non-industrial private landowners: 40%

Did you know. . .

that more than 70% of people who took at least one spring or summer trip in Minnesota rated "observing natural scenery" as the most important activity of their trip?

The Boundary Waters Canoe Area Wilderness

It is a debate that began in the 1920s when Ernest Oberholtzer, a young Harvard-educated Iowan who moved in to the area. He became the lead spokesperson for opposition to a series of dams that business mogul Edward Backus wanted to construct. The history of this 1.09 million-acre wilderness area within the Superior National Forest in northeastern Minnesota is intimately entwined with the history of the state.

Its existence and the debate that still surrounds it, represent the classic modern dilemma: development and economic interests versus the preservation of a unique wilderness area.

With the backing of Minneapolis area lawyers Sewell Tyng, Frank Hubachek, Charles Kelly, Frederick Winston as well as political support, Oberholtzer won an improbable victory.

In 1930, federal legislation protected the area, in law, as a wilderness area. In 1964, Hubert Humphrey sponsored the Wilderness Act that restricted any vehicles or the building of any structures in the area. In 1978, a new Act banned mining, logging and snowmobiles and limited the use of motorboats.

The political story of the BWCAW should not overshadow the magnificence of what *National Geographic* billed as one of its "50 Destinations of a Lifetime."

If you are wondering what the landscape looked like once the glaciers melted in the last Ice Age, you'll get a glimpse of that here. There are more than 1,500 miles of canoe routes and more than 2,150 campsites. There are literally 1,000 lakes and streams. It is also estimated to contain some 400,000 acres of old-growth forest. Despite its remoteness, it is one of the most visited parks in the country.

Did you know. . .

that there are 22 lakes within Minneapolis city limits?

FISHING

Minnesota lakes and rivers hold nearly 160 species of fish and there are 3.8 million acres of fishing waters.

- Fishable lakes: 5,493
- Fishable streams (cold and warm water): 15,000 miles
- Trout streams: 1,900 miles

The MIGHTY Mississippi

The Great Mississippi is the continent's longest river. Its influence and story are as much entwined in American fables and history as any physical feature of the country. Native Americans used it for transportation and food, and the settlers that would follow used it to establish one of the most important trading and transportation routes known to the world.

As all Minnesota schoolchildren know, the headwaters of the Mississippi are located at Lake Itasca in the Lake District in the northwestern part of the state in Clearwater County. For 575 miles, the river winds through the state, past Grand Rapids, St. Cloud, Minneapolis and St. Paul, and Winona. From there it travels for nearly another 2,000 miles before finally draining into the Gulf of Mexico. It directly traverses 10 states, but its watershed is such that it drains water through wetlands and tributaries from 32 states and two Canadian provinces, a total of 1.2 million square miles.

The Twin Cities, of course, owe their prominence to the Mississippi. Lambert's Landing in St. Paul was the last place to unload boats coming upriver, while St. Anthony Falls provided the water power for the industry that made Minneapolis "Mill City."

The port cities of Minneapolis and St. Paul lobbied very early

- Sport fish harvested:
  Panfish: 64 million pounds
  Walleye: 35 million pounds
  Northern pike: 3.2 million

Source: Minnesota Department of Natural Resources

on and very successfully for the development of the river, first to bring settlers to the state, then to transport goods to the rest of the country. Since 1866, four channel projects, as well as a number of locks and dams, have transformed Minnesota. In 1857, the port of St. Paul had more than 1,000 steamboat arrivals alone. They brought goods, of course, but they also brought people. Minnesota's population jumped accordingly, from 6,000 to more than 170,000 in 10 years. Those newcomers, and the ones following them, would transform the state into an economic powerhouse.

Today, the Mississippi basin produces 92% of the nation's agricultural exports, 78% of the world's exports in feed grains and soybeans, and most of the livestock and hogs produced nationally. Sixty percent of all grain exported from the US is shipped via the Mississippi River, a large part of that coming from Minnesota. The Mississippi's value extends beyond the economic. For Native Americans, the Mississippi (especially the confluence of the Minnesota and the Mississippi) represent a spiritual connection to the land and form part of their creation myth. Moreover, for an increasing number of Minnesotans and Americans, reclaiming, restoring, and ultimately respecting the ecological integrity of the Mississippi is a high priority.

PARK IT

The Minnesota Department of Natural Resources State Park system includes 72 state parks and recreation areas (66 parks and 6 recreation areas), 8 waysides, 11 state trails, and 56 state forest campgrounds and day-use areas.

- Total land area of state parks: 267,251 acres
- Number of miles of canoeing routes: 4,256
- Number of miles of groomed snowmobile trails: 20,000
- Number of beaches: 40
- Number of horse camp sites: 293
- Number of park visitors: 8,375,506
- Number of campers: 979,000

TAKE5 TOP FIVE
HIKING OR BIKING TRAILS

1. **The Superior Hiking Trail:** Named one of the top 10 trails in the world by *Backpacker* magazine. It covers more than 220 miles in northern Minnesota, including the beautiful North Shore of Lake Superior.

2. **Cannon Valley Trail:** Connects the southern cities of Cannon Falls, Red Wing, and Welch with a 20-mile bike trail through beautiful bluffs and valleys.

3. **Root River Trail:** Sixty miles of paved trails amidst 300-foot bluffs connects southern Minnesota cities like Lanesboro, Fountain, and Harmony.

4. **The Heartland Trail:** This 50-mile stretch takes bikers through the center cities of Minnesota, including Park Rapids, Dorset, and Walker. It meets up with other trails such as the Paul Bunyan Trail and the Migizi Trail loop.

5. **Gateway Trail:** Starts just north of the state Capitol in downtown St. Paul and runs for nearly 20 miles, ending just north of Stillwater.

Source: Minnesota Trails

TAKE 5 PAUL STAFFORD'S FIVE PLACES
TO SNAP A NATURE PHOTO

Born and raised in Minneapolis, Paul Stafford has been a professional photographer for 33 years, specializing in nature and environmental portraits. His photographs have been published in national and international newspapers, magazines, books, and calendars.

1. **Blue Mounds State Park** offers tallgrass prairie, a large variety of wildflowers, a herd of 50 bison, and a Sioux quartzite rock cliff rising 100 feet from the prairie. Early morning is a good time to photograph the rock cliff. Wildflowers bloom in June through August.

2. **Wilderness Drive in Itasca State Park** begins at the Mississippi River Headwaters and winds for another 11 miles along the undeveloped west side of Lake Itasca. Along the one-way drive are the largest white and red pine trees in Minnesota, pink lady slippers and a fire tower perfect for panoramic views of Minnesota's largest park.

3. Along the **Superior Hiking Trail** are several scenic overlooks. One of the best vantage points is at the top of Oberg Mountain. The loop trail at the top of the peak has seven overlooks featuring views of Lake Superior and the Superior National Forest. The best time of year is fall when the maples are in full color.

4. Stretching for more than 100 miles along the Minnesota border with Canada is the **Boundary Waters Canoe Area Wilderness**. When you push off into these waters, you leave far behind the trappings of civilization.

5. One of the only urban wildlife refuges in the nation is located within minutes of downtown Minneapolis. The **Minnesota Valley National Wildlife Refuge** is a gateway to 14,000 acres of habitat for bald eagles, beavers, and coyotes. The Bloomington Ferry and Rapids Lake sections are two favorites for wildlife sighting and provide an interesting landscape of dense flood plain forest, oak savannah, and prairie.

TAKE**5** FIVE BIRDS
THAT LET YOU KNOW IT IS SPRING

1. **American Kestrel**
2. **Eastern Bluebird**
3. **Eastern Phoebe**
4. **Red-winged Blackbird**
5. **American Robin**

VOYAGEURS

When President Richard Nixon created Voyageurs National Park in 1971, he stated that it should serve as a living legacy linking generation to generation and century to century. Indeed a large part of the impetus for Voyageurs was to preserve the historic waterway used by French voya-

Did you know. . .

... that Walter Palmer, notorious for his 2015 killing of Cecil the lion while on a hunting trip in Zimbabwe, hails from Minnesota? The Bloomington dentist is apparently no friend to wildlife close to home either, having been fined by the US Fish and Wildlife Service for a cover-up related to his 2006 illegal killing of a black bear in Wisconsin. In late 2015, Palmer was reported to the Minnesota Department of Natural Resources for allegedly using his vehicle to illegally herd deer on his western Minnesota property.

Did you know. . .

that the largest jack pine in the US can be found in Lake Bronson State Park? The tree stands 56 feet tall, and has a circumference of 116 inches, and a 61-foot crown spread. Minnesota is also home to the largest white spruce in the country. The tree, near Littlefork, stands 130 feet tall, has a 125-inch circumference, and a 28-foot crown spread.

TAKE**5** FIVE MOST VISITED
STATE PARKS

1. **Fort Snelling:** 959,859 visitors
2. **Gooseberry Falls:** 598,889 visitors
3. **Itasca:** 512,352 visitors
4. **Tettegouche:** 307,729 visitors
5. **Split Rock Lighthouse:** 304,576 visitors

Source: Minnesota Department of Natural Resources

geurs (licensed fur traders) to open up the northwestern United States.

The voyageurs, most of them coming out of Montreal, came to bargain with Native Americans for valuable pelts, especially the beaver. (Back in Europe, beaver hats were fetching the equivalent of $125 today.) It was a lucrative enough trade that even Minnesota's first governor, Henry Sibley was involved in it in his early years.

Voyageur National Park covers some 218,000 acres and stretches for 55 miles along the Canadian border, just east of International Falls. Water encompasses a full third of the park, so if you want the voyageur experience of traversing the route and exploring any of the more than 800 islands and much of the Kabetogama Peninsula at the center of the park (where there are no roads), you'll have to bring or rent a boat. You can be a voyageur!

They said it

"The whole surface of the State is literally begemmed with innumerable lakes...Their picturesque beauty and loveliness, with their pebbly bottoms, transparent waters, wooded shores and sylvan associations must be seen to be appreciated."

— Part of a promotional campaign to draw in settlers.
Guide to the Lands of the First Division of the Saint Paul and Pacific Railroad Company. Main Line, 5, 6 (St. Paul, 1870)

Culture

From F. Scott Fitzgerald, Sinclair Lewis, and Louise Erdrich to Bob Dylan, Prince, Charles Schulz, and the Coen brothers, the Gopher State has inspired generations of creative people.

Minnesotans are blessed with a vibrant arts, entertainment and culture scene. The Twin Cities metro area ranks among the nation's leaders in theater attendance, and also boasts a number of top-flight art museums.

Strong support for arts and culture is found throughout the state. You can, of course, see Shakespeare at the Guthrie Theater in Minneapolis, but also catch an Ibsen play in tiny Lanesboro in southern Minnesota. Likewise, the fine arts are displayed in galleries from Grand Marais to Moorhead to Rochester.

The arts are for all seasons in Minnesota—they have to be, as you need something to help make it through the winter. You can get creative on a frozen lake in the middle of January at the Art Shanty Projects, celebrate spring in a massive May puppet pageant, or listen to the blues in late summer on Lake Superior.

Minnesotans are committed to the arts, and two-thirds of the population attends a cultural event at least once a year. In 2008, voters passed the Clean Water, Land and Legacy Amendment which raised the state's sales tax to help fund environmental, recreational and arts projects. The result was an estimated $50 million in additional funding for the arts in Minnesota. The state is also home to some impressive foundations — which underwrite everything from theaters to music festivals to cultural organizations.

Minnesotans are a sporty bunch. The state is well-known as a paradise for anglers and hunters, and amateur sports, from soccer, basketball, track and field, baseball and hockey to swimming and lacrosse all have their devotees. The National Sport Center in Blaine bills itself as the "World's Largest Amateur Sports and Meeting Facility," and for good reason: its 52 grass soccer fields make it the Guinness-certified world's largest soccer complex.

Those who prefer their sports from the comfort of an arena or stadium seat are also well-served. There are pro baseball, football, basketball and hockey squads in the Twin Cities, and sports fans have been richly rewarded with athletic thrills from the likes of Fran Tarkenton, Alan Page, Harmon Killebrew, Rod Carew, Kirby Puckett, Joe Mauer and Kevin Garnett, to name just a few of the stars who have played locally.

THE BUSINESS OF CULTURE
- Number of artists: 30,000
- Number of arts organizations: 1,600

Did you know. . .

that the Andrews Sisters (Patty, Maxene, and LaVerne) were born and raised in Minneapolis? The sisters recorded 700 songs, sold 90 million records, and made 17 movies. The height of their popularity was the 1940s when they were known as "America's War-time Sweethearts" and inspired soldiers stationed abroad and folks on the homefront, with well-crafted optimistic songs. Patty Andrews, the youngest of the sisters, died in 2013 at the age of 94, having been preceded by sisters Maxene who died in 1995, and LaVerne who died in 1967 at age 55.

They said it

"When the show started, it was something funny to do with my friends, and then it became an achievement that I hoped would be successful, and now it's a good way of life."

— Garrison Keillor, from the *A Prairie Home Companion* website

- Amount spent per trip by "cultural tourists": $614 (average travelers spend $425).
- Annual economic impact of culture on the state: $1 billion

MUSIC

From the World War II-era Andrews Sisters to 1960s Billboard chart-topping crooner Bobby Vee to Bob Dylan, Prince and 1980s indie-rock legends Hüsker Dü and the Replacements, Minnesota has produced some of the nation's musical greats.

Bobby Vee

Vee, an early 1960s teen-idol, was born Robert Thomas Velline in Fargo, ND, in 1943. In the late 1950s, he moved to Minneapolis, adopted the Vee moniker and proceeded to reel off a series of hits. All told, he scored 14 top-40 hits, including such smashes as "Devil or Angel," "Rubber Ball," and "Take Good Care of My Baby."

In addition to being a star in his own right, Vee has kept some interesting company. In 1959, the plane carrying Buddy Holly, Richie Valens, and The Big Bopper to an Iowa concert crashed, killing all on board. Somebody was needed to fill in for the show, and a 15-year-

Did you know. . .

that Minnesota resident Hazel Frederick made her unwitting television debut during the opening credits of the *Mary Tyler Moore Show*? Frederick is the puzzled shopper in the green coat who watches as Moore flings her hat in the air.

old Vee—who had recently formed a band and knew all of Holly's songs—answered the call. The concert catapulted the young singer to fame; four years later Vee recorded a tribute album to his idol called *I Remember Buddy Holly*.

Vee was also associated with another rock legend, a Mr. Bob Zimmerman (aka Bob Dylan) who played piano for Vee's band, The Shadows. According to Vee, Dylan was a "wild card" who had great energy and obvious talent, but wasn't much of a piano player

TAKE5 FIVE HOLLYWOOD TYPES
FROM MINNESOTA

1. **James Arness (1923-2011).** Arness was born and raised in Minneapolis and began his career as a local radio announcer in 1945. He appeared in a number of movies and television shows, and was best known for playing Marshal Matt Dillon on Gunsmoke, a series that ran from 1955-1975, making it the longest-running dramatic series ever produced.

2. **Jessica Lange (1949-).** Born in Cloquet, Lange grew up in several towns in Minnesota and briefly studied art at the University of Minnesota before leaving for New York and Paris (where she studied mime). Lange's first movie was the 1976 remake of *King Kong*, and she went on to star in such films as *Tootsie, Frances, The Postman Always Rings Twice, Titus* and *Cape Fear*. Lange has won two best-actress Academy Awards and has appeared in a number of plays in New York and London.

3. **The Andersons: Louie (1953-) and Loni (1945-).** They aren't related, but they are Minnesotans. Comic Louie Anderson grew up the son of an abusive alcoholic in a poor St. Paul family. He has served as host of *Family Feud*, created the animated series *Life With Louie*, is the author of three books and a veteran of hundreds

("He played really well in the key of C, but that was about it"). Dylan stayed with the Shadows for only a few months before leaving for New York.

Vee continued to tour well into the 2000s, playing with a band that included two of his sons, and one of his nephews. His final album, *The Adobe Sessions*, was released in 2014, and was a tribute to some of the long-time Minnesota resident's favorite songs; it was recorded while Vee battled Alzheimer's disease.

of stand-up comedy performances. He also starred in The Louie Show, a 1990s sitcom that lasted only six episodes and cast its star as a Duluth psychotherapist.

Loni Anderson was born in St. Paul, grew up in Roseville, and attended the University of Minnesota. She has appeared in a variety of television shows and movies, and is best known for playing Jennifer, the blonde bombshell receptionist on the late '70s sitcom *WKRP in Cincinnati*.

4. **Winona Ryder (1971-).** Named after Winona, Minnesota, where she was born, Ryder's real last name is Horowitz. Ryder moved to Petaluma, CA, when she was a 10-year-old and made her film debut in 1986 with *Lucas*. Since then she has starred in numerous films including *Little Women, The Crucible,* and *Girl, Interrupted*.

5. **Josh Hartnett (1978-).** Born in San Franciso but raised in St. Paul, Hartnett graduated from Minneapolis's South High School. Hartnett is an actor-producer who has starred in such films as *Black Hawk Down* and *Pearl Harbor*.

His Purple Majesty

If a buoyant economy can be said to raise all boats, so, too, does the presence of genius raise the stock of a place in the minds of its residents. Although Prince's musical brilliance could have been realized in many places, it evolved and came to fruition in Minneapolis, nurtured by homegrown institutions and the city's landscapes. Local genius-artists who see Minnesota as their home but the world as their stage are Prince's progeny — he's proof you can make it big without leaving the 10,000 Lakes behind.

Prince, born Prince Rogers Nelson in 1958 in Minneapolis, was named after his father John Nelson's jazz band, the Prince Rogers Band. Prince learned to play guitar at a young age and formed his first band, Grand Central, while in junior high school.

Prince's first album came out in 1978 and since then he has produced dozens of them, in addition to being a prolific writer and producer on behalf of others. In the 1980s, Prince tended a musical hothouse that generated stars, including The Time, Vanity 6, and Sheila E. The music had a funk, rock, pop, and new wave appeal and came to be known as the Minneapolis Sound.

Prince has numerous hits to his credit; his high-water mark commercially is represented by *Purple Rain*, the soundtrack to the 1984 movie of the same name. The album spent 24 straight weeks at No.1 on the Billboard album chart, sold more than 13 million copies and won two Grammies. Prince has also garnered widespread critical acclaim, and is considered one of the leading forces in popular music over the last several decades.

"I am just like anyone else, I need love and water," Prince once told an MTV interviewer. "I live in a small town and I always will," he said. "I can walk around and be me. That's all I want to be, that's all I ever tried to be." Minnesotans have had the pleasure of watching one of the country's great musical artists come to terms with precisely that.

Prince has always fought for his public identity, and it's quite an identity: a black man in a mostly white state who stands just over 5-feet-tall, sports a wonderfully coiffed head of hair and a barely-there mustache. And then there are the clothes. And yet, Prince's music has transcended race, gender, and even generation. His music crosses all kinds of lines, and his stated influences include James Brown, Miles Davis, Carlos Santana, and Joni Mitchell.

Prince has always prided himself on his independence and has chafed at being beholden to a record label or to corporate interests. He doesn't shill for himself on late-night television, either. And, memorably, there was that business in the 1990s when he changed his name to a cryptic symbol and so was dubbed "The Artist Formerly Known as Prince."

Evidence of the Prince legend is found in the strangest places throughout his hometown, from late night haunts to early morning breakfast joints, and there is usually a story attached. Him running into estranged bandmate and friend André Cymone in a Minneapolis disco, for instance, and forcing Cymone to take the song "Dance Electric" to help patch up their relationship. Naturally, the song became a hit. Then, of course, there is Paisley Park Studios, the 55,000-square-foot sound and recording stage in Minneapolis, where Prince will offer impromptu performances, including serenading Madonna following a 2015 concert of hers in St. Paul.

After lying low for several years, in 2014-15 an afro-sporting Prince played high-profile gigs in the US and abroad, and made a number of TV appearances, including one at the 2015 Grammys. Still, he remains enigmatic and elusive, with an ambivalent relationship to the Internet and social media. He also remains a Minnesotan. F. Scott Fitzgerald left the state when he was 24, Sinclair Lewis when he was 17, and Bob Dylan at 18. Prince, despite an interlude in California, has remained in his hometown of Minneapolis, and many see this choice as a validation of the city, and of state of Minnesota.

Bob Dylan, The Early Years

If you've ever wanted to hear what Duluth-born and Hibbing-raised Robert Zimmerman (Bob Dylan) sounded like when he was a complete unknown, head to the Minnesota History Center in St. Paul. Before Dylan moved to New York in early 1961, he attended the University of Minnesota and played at coffeehouses around Dinkytown, a neighborhood near the university. It was during this period that he adopted the last name "Dylan," an homage to Welsh poet Dylan Thomas.

TAKE5 FIVE MINNESOTA MUSIC FESTIVALS

1. **Minnesota Orchestra's Sommerfest.** The music spills out of Orchestra Hall and onto Peavey Plaza every July in Minneapolis. The event hosts a mix of symphonic, chamber, rock, and jazz. The outdoor events are free.

2. **Basilica Block Party.** "Your Ticket to Musical Redemption" happens in July at the Basilica of Saint Mary in downtown Minneapolis. It's a fundraiser for the Basilica and features rock and indie music acts.

3. **WE Fest.** A major country music festival, featuring the likes of Kenny Chesney and Keith Urban, WE Fest takes place the first weekend in August at Detroit Lakes. It's been going since 1983.

4. **Minnesota Bluegrass and Old-Time Music Festival.** This is one of four annual festivals presented by the Minnesota Bluegrass & Old-Time Music Association, and every August it draws a picking-and -grinning crowd to a campground near Richmond.

5. **Bayfront Blues Festival.** Held in Duluth, the festival has featured more than 300 bands at the Bayfront every August since 1989.

They said it

"You're pretty much ruled by nature up there. You have to sort of fall into line with that, regardless of how you're feeling that day or what you might want to do with your life or what you think about."

— Bob Dylan, in a 1984 *Rolling Stone* interview with Kurt Loder, when asked about growing up in Hibbing in the 1950s

A 12-song recording of one of Dylan's impromptu performances at an apartment in 1960 is now part of the Minnesota Historical Society's (MHS) library, and one can hear excerpts from the "Minnesota Party Tape" at the Minnesota History Center. The tape was made by Minneapolis resident Cleve Pettersen on a reel-to-reel tape recorder that he had just bought. He was looking for a local folk singer to sing songs into his new machine, and Dylan agreed.

In 2004, Pettersen donated the original tape to the Historical Society.

Those wishing to truly explore Dylan's roots can head north to the mining town of Hibbing where Dylan spent most of his childhood. His father helped run the family appliance store, and Bob Zimmerman grew up in a modest but comfortable house on Seventh Avenue East.

Did you know. . .

that Minneapolis-St. Paul ranks seventh nationwide for recreational opportunities, according to the *Places Rated Almanac*? The Twin Cities boast more than 150 golf courses and feature 63,000 acres of recreation areas, 192,000 acres of lakes and rivers, more than 530 movie theater screens, two zoos, three amusement parks, and nearly 150 professional sporting events annually.

FIRST NAMES

First Avenue, which bills itself as "Your Downtown Danceteria Since 1970," was Prince's regular venue in the 1980s, and has been integral to the Twin Cities' music scene since its 1970 opening. Over the decades, musicians who have played the Art Deco-themed former Greyhound bus depot have included Joe Cocker (who played the night the club opened), Frank Zappa, Ike and Tina Turner, The Kinks, The Allman Brothers, John Lee Hooker, James Brown, The Ramones, U2, REM,

TAKE*5* FIVE MADE IN MINNESOTA
MOVIES

1. *North Country* (2005). Directed by Niki Caro and starring Charlize Theron, Woody Harrelson, and Frances McDormand. Filmed in the mining town of Chisholm and other Minnesota locations.

2. *Fargo* (1996). Directed by Ethan and Joel Coen. Minnesota locations included Minneapolis, Edina, Brainerd, St. Louis Park, Stillwater, and Minneapolis-St. Paul International Airport. *A Serious Man* (2009) was also filmed in the Twin Cities.

3. *Jingle All the Way* (1996). Directed by Brian Levant and starring Arnold Schwarzenegger, Sinbad, and Phil Hartman. Minnesota locations include the Mall of America, the 7th Place Mall in downtown St. Paul, and other Twin Cities locations.

4. *Mallrats* (1995). Directed by Kevin Smith and starring Shannen Doherty, Jeremy London, and Jason Lee. Filmed at the Eden Prairie Center mall in Eden Prairie.

5. *Grumpy Old Men* (1993) and *Grumpier Old Men* (1995). Directed by Donald Petrie and Howard Deutch, and starring Jack Lemmon, Walter Matthau, and Ann Margret. Minnesota is effectively a character itself in these two comedies set in rural Wabasha, and filmed in Wabasha and a number of other locations around the state.

David Byrne, and Green Day. In the 1990s and 2000s, First Avenue has continued to host local and touring acts, as well as embracing DJ culture. Current Minnesota bands that have played the famed venue include Atmosphere and Tapes N Tapes. In recognition of its 40 years in business, Minneapolis Mayor R.T. Ryback declared April 3, 2010, "First Avenue Day."

TAKE5 FIVE MINNESOTA
BALLET COMPANIES

1. **Minnesota Dance Theatre and Dance Institute.** Founded in 1962 by Loyce Houlton, MDT is a leading regional dance organization and presents an eclectic range of new and classic dance. *The Nutcracker Fantasy* is a much-beloved holiday treat. The Dance Institute represents the 2006 union of the schools of the MDT and Ballet Arts Minnesota. The MDT is based at the Hennepin Center for the Arts in downtown Minneapolis. www.mndance.org.

2. **James Sewell Ballet.** Founded in New York by James Sewell and Sally Rouse, the innovative and critically acclaimed JSB company came to the Twin Cities in 1992 and performs at the Hennepin Theater Trust in Minneapolis. www.jsballet.org.

3. **Ballet Minnesota/Classical Ballet Academy.** St. Paul-based Ballet Minnesota was founded in 1988 by Andrew and Cheryl Rist and is the performing company of the Classical Ballet Academy. www.balletminnesota.org.

4. **Continental Ballet Company.** Continental was founded by Riet Velthuisen in 1988 and is based in Bloomington. It offers a range of classic ballet performances, as well as education and outreach. www.continentalballet.com.

5. **Minnesota Ballet.** The Minnesota Ballet is a 14-member company based in Duluth. Founded in 1965, it has a diverse repertoire and tours nationally. www.minnesotaballet.org.

CRITICAL ACCLAIM

The 1980s was a banner decade for rock music in the Twin Cities. *Rolling Stone Magazine's* "100 Greatest Albums of the '80s" included five by Minnesota artists:

TAKE5 ADAM GRANGER'S FIVE PIECES
OF *A PRAIRIE HOME COMPANION* TRIVIA

Musician Adam Granger was one of the founding members of the Powdermilk Biscuit Band on National Public Radio's *A Prairie Home Companion*. He moved to Minnesota in 1975 after working with a travelling band from Nashville and playing bluegrass in Oklahoma. Shortly after arriving in the Twin Cities, the show's creator, Garrison Keillor, heard Granger play at the Coffeehouse Extempore, a renowned folk venue in the West Bank neighborhood of Minneapolis. Granger played with the band from 1976 to 1979. Since then, he has guest-hosted the show five times and has also written for it. He still does, on occasion. "I'm on once a year or so these days," he says, "which is just right." Today, *A Prairie Home Companion* is heard by more than 4 million listeners each week on some 590 public radio stations.

1. **The first tour.** Garrison Keillor's first "tour" was in 1973. Keillor, musicians Bill Hinkley and Judy Larson, and engineer Jerry Vanek floated down the upper Mississippi River from Lake Bemidji to Grand Rapids in two canoes. Garrison taped commentaries on a portable reel-to-reel tape recorder (including nature sounds like beavers slapping their tails, which were actually created by slapping canoe paddles against the water). When they stopped at night, Vanek ran to the post office and mailed the "dispatches" to Minnesota Public Radio.

2. **The great outdoors.** In the 1970s, the show was sometimes performed outdoors, usually in the sculpture garden of the Minnesota Science Museum. The decision to do the show indoors or outdoors was made one hour before airtime. Sometimes, colorful characters

- *Purple Rain* — Prince (No.2)
- *Let it Be* — The Replacements (No.15)
- *1999* — Prince (No.16)
- *Dirty Mind* — Prince (No.18)
- *Zen Arcade* — Hüsker Dü (No.33)

came in off the street and extemporaneously joined the show. One blues harp player actually made it to the stage, briefly accompanying the "News from Lake Wobegon" segment.

3. **Spontaneous guests.** In the early days, Keillor would sometimes spontaneously invite people he heard during the week to be on the show. The house band never knew quite what to expect in these situations, but it was usually a successful venture. Rehearsals were often done in the hallways during the show.

4. **Bats and plaster.** When *A Prairie Home Companion* moved into St. Paul's World Theater (now the Fitzgerald Theater), there was a false ceiling covering the second balcony. During shows, bats came through holes in the ceiling and swooped down on the audience and performers. After the ceiling was removed, but before the building was renovated, chunks of plaster occasionally fell from the ceiling. No injuries were ever reported. Coincidentally, the World Theater was owned by the Dworskys, whose son, Rich, is now the show's music director.

5. **Extras.** Robert Altman's movie *A Prairie Home Companion*, filmed in 2006, was populated with extras who were regulars on the show and who were added to the movie for verisimilitude. They included Bill Hinkley, Judy Larson, Adam Granger, Bob Douglas, Dan Newton, John Koerner, Jon Pankake, Butch Thompson, Dick Rees, and Peter Ostroushko.

NAME DROPPERS: JOEL AND ETHAN COEN

The Brothers Coen, who grew up in the Minneapolis suburb of St. Louis Park, rank among the top filmmakers of their generation. Joel (born 1954) and Ethan (born 1957) have, since the mid-1980s, written, produced, and directed more than a dozen movies. Some of their films, like the Oscar-winning *No Country for Old Men* (2007) are very dark, while others, such as *Raising Arizona* (1987), verge on slapstick. Then there is *Fargo* (1996), which leaves audience members unsure whether they should be laughing, crying, or covering their eyes.

The Coen oeuvre has particular resonance for Minnesotans, as the brothers enjoy playing with the names of Twin Cities celebrities. To wit:

- **Ron Meshbesher**. In *A Serious Man* (2009), protagonist Larry Gopnik's brother is advised to hire lawyer Ron Meshbesher. The name is hardly random; Meshbesher is a Twin Cities lawyer who has handled a number of high-profile cases and is frequently seen in television ads for his firm, Meshbesher and Spence.
- **Rabbi Marshak**. In *A Serious Man*, the character Rabbi Marshak, who counsels 13-year-old Danny Gopnik after his Bar Mitzvah, shares the same last name as Marvin Marshak, a physics professor at the University of Minnesota where the brothers' dad, Ed Coen, taught economics.
- **Ruth Brin**. Also in *A Serious Man*, the quick line "Ruth Brin's mother is in the hospital" is no doubt a nod to local poet and Jewish liturgist Ruth Brin, who died in September 2009.
- **Jerry Lundegaard**. In *Fargo*, Jerry Lundegaard is the name of the car salesman played by William H. Macy. The name is borrowed from Bob Lundegaard, film critic for the *Minneapolis Star* and *Tribune* from 1973-86. The double "a" in Lundegaard is highly unusual. When *Fargo* premiered in Minneapolis, Lundegaard was invited to the screening and notes, "After the movie, one of them was standing in the lobby, and I went up to him and said, 'My lawyers will call you in the morning.' He just shrugged and said, 'It's a very common name.'"
- **Bill Diehl**. Twenty minutes into *Fargo*, Jerry Lundegaard is advised to "go to Midwest Federal. Talk to old Bill Diehl." Bill Diehl was the movie

editor for the *St. Paul Pioneer Press-Dispatch* during the Coens' formative years, and was often heard on WCCO radio pitching for an Oldsmobile dealership. Diehl had interviewed the Coens shortly after the 1984 release of their debut film, *Blood Simple* (as had Bob Lundegaard).

TAKE5 FIVE MINNESOTA THEATERS
THAT AREN'T IN THE TWIN CITIES

1. **Jon Hassler Theater.** The company performs in a former International Harvester implement dealership in Plainview, where the theater's namesake grew up. The theater has produced a number of adaptations of Hassler's novels, including *Grand Opening, Simon's Night, Dear James,* and *Rookery Blues.* Jon Hassler (1993-2008) often wrote about life in small town Minnesota, and for many years was writer in residence at St. John's University in Collegeville. www.jonhasslertheater.org.

2. **Commonweal Theatre Company.** The Commonweal is known for its annual Henrik Ibsen Festival, a nod to the Nordic heritage of area residents. In 2007, the Lanesboro-based company built a $3.5-million facility that included seats reclaimed from the original Guthrie Theater in Minneapolis. www.commonwealtheatre.org.

3. **Paul Bunyan Playhouse.** Located in Bemidji in Lake Country, the Paul Bunyan Playhouse opened in 1951 and is the longest continuously-running summer-stock theater company in Minnesota. www.paulbunyanplayhouse.com.

4. **Theatre L'Homme Dieu.** The theater debuted in 1961 and is near Alexandria in the Lakes Area. In the summer of 2009, the theater partnered with other professional regional theaters, to bring audiences a range of comedies and musicals. www.tlhd.org.

5. **Center for the Arts.** The Fergus Falls theater features a mighty Wurlitzer theater pipe organ that rises up in center stage. The center brings live theater, movies, music, dance, visual arts exhibitions and festivals, numerous workshops, and literary events to the western part of the state. www.fergusarts.org.

THEATER

Minnesotans are among the nation's most avid theater-goers, and the Twin Cities rank second only to New York in per-capita theater seats. There is an almost endless variety of theater in the state: you can catch a musical at the Chanhassen Dinner Theatres while dining on pork chops, walleye or spaghetti; enjoy a production of the Children's Theatre Company (one of the three largest such troupes in the world),

Bio F. Scott Fitzgerald

F. Scott Fitzgerald left the city of St. Paul in 1919 when he was only 23, but the imprint of the city on him and, in turn, his imprint on the city (and the state) remain huge. Writers and admirers stroll the old Fitzgerald addresses (481 Laurel Ave., since named a National Literary Landmark; 509 Holly Ave., 593 Summit Ave., 599 Summit Ave., and 626 Goodrich Ave.), gazing into the same windows the author of *The Great Gatsby* must have once gazed out of himself.

Named after "Star Spangled Banner" writer Francis Scott Key (a distant cousin of his father), Fitzgerald was born into a wealthy and ambitious St. Paul family. Although his father was from Maryland, the money that would allow a young Fitzgerald to go to private boarding school in New Jersey and later to Princeton came from his mother, Mary (Mollie) McQuillan, whose father made his fortune as a wholesale grocer in St. Paul.

Fitzgerald's first novel, *This Side of Paradise*, was published in 1919 after two earlier rejections. Completed in St. Paul, it tells the story of Amory Blaine, a young Midwesterner brimming with promise who, like Fitzgerald, attends Princeton. Blaine falls in love with a New York City debutante, but is rejected because he is too poor.

In his own life, Fitzgerald's engagement to Zelda Sayre (the daughter of a Montgomery, Alabama judge whom Fitzgerald met while stationed in the Army) was broken off by Sayre. She was concerned about Fitzgerald's prospects, and was being courted by others. So convinced was Fitzgerald of his destiny of fame and fortune, that he encouragement on his publisher, Scribner, to get *This Side of Paradise* out early so that he might collect his rightful dividend. The novel or take in a touring Broadway show at one of the Hennepin theater Trust's historic venues. Small independent theatre companies such as the Jungle, Minnesota Opera, Mixed Blood, and Penumbra offer an eclectic mix of classic and contemporary performances. And a trip to the theater need not be a snooty or sedentary affair: the Bryant Lake Bowl in Minneapolis is a bowling alley, restaurant, bar and theatre all rolled into one.

became a huge hit for and launched Fitzgerald's career. The following year, Sayre and Fitzgerald were married at St. Patrick's Cathedral in New York City, and in 1921, their only child, a daughter named Scottie, was born. Together, F. Scott and Zelda would become symbols of the Jazz Age and one of the most celebrated couples in American literary history.

In four glorious novels, Fitzgerald was able to cut to the very heart of the American Dream. He captured that great yearning for power, prosperity, and recognition in a way that no other writer has before or since. *The Great Gatsby*, which was published in 1925 and considered a failure during Fitzgerald's lifetime, remains a classic and is a staple of high school and college reading lists. In addition to his explorations of New York-area debutantes and dilettantes, Fitzgerald mined the experiences of his Minnesota youth for a series of short stories. In the *Basil & Josephine Stories*, Fitzgerald describes the St. Paul Winter Carnival, the Minnesota State Fair, and the White Bear Yacht Club. Indeed, his residence in Minnesota was the longest Fitzgerald lived in any one place during his short life. In addition to writing novels and short fiction, Fitzgerald wrote a number of film scripts, most of which never saw the light of day. *Three Comrades* (1938), based on Erich Maria Remarque's novel, did make it to the screen, and Fitzgerald also briefly worked on the script for *Gone With the Wind.*

Debt and prosperity, excess and indulgence, fame and infamy characterized the life of Fitzgerald and his wife, Zelda. When he died in Los Angeles as a result of alcoholism at the age of 44, the boy whose first short story had appeared in the St. Paul Academy newspaper *Then and Now* (now called *The Rubicon*), and who had his first play staged by the local Elizabethan Dramatic Club when he was 14, belonged to the world.

TAKE 5 FIVE QUINTESSENTIAL
MINNESOTA AUTHORS

1. **Margaret Culkin Banning (1891-1982).** Born in Buffalo, this women's rights advocate and bestselling author wrote nearly 400 essays and short stories about social issues, as well as 36 novels, including *Country Club People* and *The First Woman*. Banning served two terms in the Minnesota State Senate.

2. **Maud Hart Lovelace (1892-1980).** A native of Mankato, Lovelace is beloved throughout the state for her *Betsy-Tacy* children's books. The first in the series, which Lovelace based on her own life as a 5-year-old, was published in 1940. She published a *Betsy-Tacy* book a year, ending the series in 1955 with Betsy's marriage. Lovelace's other novels include *The Black Angels* (1926) and *Early Candlelight* (1929).

3. **Ole E. Rølvaag (1876-1931).** Rølvaag was born and raised in rural Norway and came to the U.S. as a 20-year-old. He wrote novels, essays and texts about the Norwegian immigrant experience, and was for many years a professor of Norwegian language and literature at St. Olaf College in Northfield.

4. **Robert Bly (1926-).** Minnesota's first poet laureate was born in Madison in western Minnesota. He is the author of dozens of books of poetry, as well as translations and non-fiction titles. Bly is also well-known as an activist, a social critic, and a pioneer in the men's movement, during which he wrote the widely influential 1990 book *Iron John: A Book about Men*.

5. **Louise Erdrich (1954-).** Born in Little Falls to a Ojibwe Indian mother and German-American father, Erdrich is author of many acclaimed novels, including *The Plague of Doves* (2008) and *Love Medicine* (1984), which won the National Books Critics Circle Award. Erdrich collaborated on some of her innovative non-linear fiction with her late husband, Michael Dorris. Erdrich's writing often deals with themes related to the Native American experience, and she is owner of Birchbark Books in Minneapolis. In 2015, she received the Library of Congress Prize for American Fiction.

HENNEPIN THEATRE TRUST

Hennepin Avenue in Minneapolis was once home to more than 30 theaters, but now only a few remain. The Hennepin Theatre Trust has been instrumental in the restoration and renovation of these historic jewels. For a modest $5, architecture, show business and history buffs can join a public tour of the three historic Trust theaters. www.hennepintheatretrust.org.

The State Theater (1921), 805 Hennepin Avenue. When it opened, the 2,200 seat State was considered among the nation's grandest and most technologically sophisticated theaters. It served as a movie theater until 1978, spent a decade as a church and then, in the late 1980s, received a major renovation, opening in its current form in 1991. It hosts touring theatrical shows, concerts, and comedy and spoken-word performances.

The Orpheum (1921), 910 Hennepin Avenue. The Orpheum, at nearly 2,600 seats, was one of the biggest vaudeville houses in the nation and hosted the Marx Brothers in its first week. Later, George Burns, Jack Benny, and big bands, such as Benny Goodman, Tommy Dorsey, and Count Basie took to the Orpheum stage. The Orpheum has also served as a venue for touring theatrical productions and as a movie house. It was renovated in 1993 after having been purchased from then-owners Bob Dylan and his brother, David Zimmerman. The Orpheum is often the site of touring Broadway shows such as *The Lion King, Wicked,* and *Jersey Boys.*

Did you know. . .

that the Twin Cities are home to two professional orchestras: The Minnesota Orchestra and the St. Paul Chamber Orchestra, the only full-time professional chamber orchestra in the country? Minnesota classical music fans can also catch the acclaimed Minnesota Beethoven Festival, which happens every summer in the Mississippi River town of Winona.

Pantages Theater (1916), 710 Hennepin Avenue. The Pantages seats 1,000 and opened in 1916 as a vaudeville house. It went through several renovations and reincarnations until becoming a top movie theater in 1961 (*Spartacus* was the debut screening). The theater was closed between 1984 and 1996, and then purchased and renovated. It re-opened in 2002, and presents a variety of music, theater, and dance performances.

Hennepin Stages Theater (1930s), 824 Hennepin Avenue. The Hennepin Stages consists of a 240-seat main floor theater and a 230-seat upstairs venue. The building was formerly the flagship store of local paint and wallpaper baron, Hirshfield's and was nearly turned into a porn shop before the city of Minneapolis assisted in its purchase and renovation.

THE GUTHRIE THEATER

The Guthrie Theater, a Minneapolis icon, opened in 1963. In the late 1950s, Anglo-Irish director Sir Tyrone Guthrie pitched the idea of opening a theater that had its own resident-acting company to a number of cities across the United States. Guthrie, who was also founding artistic director of Canada's Stratford Festival in 1953, chose the Twin Cities because he said the community showed enthusiasm for the project. It didn't hurt that a steering committee helped raise $900,000 for the theater. Its original site was behind the Walker Art Center, on land donated by the T. B. Walker Foundation.

The Guthrie got off to a bang with Jessica Tandy starring in *Hamlet* in its first production. The first summer season saw four productions supported by a minimal staff; the theater now employs more than 900 people per year. In 2006, a new multi-stage theater opened on the banks of the Mississippi River. Designed by French architect Jean

Did you know. . .

that once every 10 years the Minneapolis Institute of Arts hosts Foot in the Door, an unjuried open exhibition open to all Minnesota artists? In 2010, the MIA received nearly 5,000 submissions.

Nouvel, the complex includes three stages: a classic thrust stage for grand-scale productions; a proscenium stage for more intimate works; and a studio theater for developing new work. The elegant theater complex, which mixes daring space-age elements with a tip of the hat to its industrial river-front neighbors, has spectacular views and features a full-service restaurant.

The 2010 production of *The Tragedy of Macbeth* represented the Guthrie's 50th Shakespeare play. A number of well-known actors began their careers in Guthrie Shakespeare plays, including Dianne Wiest, Frank Langella, William H. Macy, Val Kilmer, Patti LuPone, David Hyde Pierce, and Julianne Moore.

TAKE5 SUSAN MARIE SWANSON'S
FIVE MINNESOTA PICTURE BOOKS

Susan Marie Swanson is a poet, teacher, and picture-book writer. She is the author of the 2009 Caldecott award-winning *The House in the Night*, as well as a number of other books, including *The First Thing My Mama Told Me* and *To Be Like the Sun*. She lives in St. Paul with her family.

1. *Antler, Bear, Canoe: A Northwoods Alphabet Year* by Betsy Bowen (Houghton Mifflin 1991). Woodcut illustrations portray elements of northern life from A to Z.

2. *Song of the Water Boatman & Other Pond Poems* by Joyce Sidman, illustrated by Becky Prange (Houghton Mifflin 2005). Pond life through the seasons.

3. *Two Old Potatoes and Me* by John Coy, illustrated by Carolyn Fisher (Alfred A. Knopf 2003). Two rotting potatoes yield a bountiful new crop of spuds for a girl and her father.

4. *Winter is the Warmest Season* by Lauren Stringer (Harcourt, 2006). A boy explains how winter, not summer, is the warmest time of year.

5. *Harriet and Walt* by Nancy Carlson (Carolrhoda 2004; originally published 1982). Harriet's little brother tags along to play in the snow in one of a series of books set in different seasons.

THE ART SCENE

Minnesota is home to dozens of museums and galleries, the three biggies are the Walker Art Center, the Minneapolis Institute of Arts, and the Weisman Art Museum.

TAKE 5 FIVE WINTER EVENTS THAT
HELP MINNESOTANS GET THROUGH IT

1. **St. Paul Winter Carnival.** The carnival has been part of the winterscape since 1886, when business leaders attempted to disprove a New York reporter's description of their city as "another Siberia, unfit for human habitation in the winter." The winter fest includes two parades, ice-and snow-sculpting contests, a giant snow slide, and, occasionally, an ice castle. www.winter-carnival.com.

2. **Art Shanty Projects.** The four-weekend exhibition comprises performance, architecture, science, art, video, literature, survivalism, and karaoke. In sum, it's part sculpture park, part artist residency, and part social experiment. The wild installation of ice shanties on Medicine Lake, just west of Minneapolis, is inspired by the traditional ice-fishing houses that dot the state's lakes in winter. www.artshantyprojects.org.

3. **John Beargrease Sled Dog Marathon.** The race starts in Duluth and honors John Beargrease, a Native American who delivered mail between Two Harbors and Grand Marais in the late 1800s, using sled dogs in the winter. Mushers compete to qualify for the Alaskan Iditarod. www.beargrease.com.

4. **Grumpy Old Men Festival.** The Wabasha event is named after the film of the same name. It features an ice-fishing competition, pet pageant, and motorcycle demos on ice, among other family-friendly fare.

5. **Eelpout Festival.** The annual ice-fishing derby is held on Leech Lake in Walker. It celebrates an ugly bottom-feeding fish that apparently rises to the surface in the winter to spawn. www.eelpoutfestival.com.

Did you know. . .

that the illustrator for the Harry Potter series of books is Minnesota artist Mary GrandPre, a graduate of the Minneapolis College of Art and Design? In addition to crafting the likeness of everyone's favorite boy wizard, GrandPre has illustrated a number of other children's books and has worked commercially.

Walker Art Center. Established in 1927, the museum's focus on modern art began in the 1940s, and the Walker is now recognized as one of the nation's premier venues for multi-disciplinary modern and contemporary art. The Walker has built an impressive collection that includes works by Pablo Picasso, Henry Moore, Edward Hopper, Georgia O'Keeffe, Andy Warhol, George Segal, Claes Oldenburg and Matthew Barney. In addition to the visual arts, the Walker offers performing arts, film, and educational programs. The Minneapolis Sculpture Garden, one of the nation's largest urban sculpture parks, opened in 1988 adjacent to the center. The Walker's recent expansion was designed by Swiss architects Jacques Herzog and Pierre de Meuron, the team that designed the main stadium for the 2008 Beijing Olympics and a new facility for San Francisco's de Young Museum. www.walkerart.org.

Did you know. . .

that the tiny town of New York Mills hosts the Great American Think-Off, a national philosophy competition where contestants submit a 750-word essay pondering a philosophical question. Four finalists get an all-expense-paid trip to the final debate in June. It began in 1993 with the question, "The Nature of Humankind: Inherently Good or Inherently Evil?" A priest, newspaper editor, 15-year-old cheerleader, and former tribal police officer made such strong arguments that the audience couldn't decide, leaving the question of humankind's essential nature unresolved. A recent question was "Is it more ethical to compromise than to stick to one's principles?" Compromise won.

The Minneapolis Institute of Arts (MIA). The MIA has some modern architecture of its own to tout: a wing designed by Princeton architect Michael Graves in 2006. The institute—which houses more than 80,000 objects—had its origins in the Minneapolis Society of Fine Arts, established in 1883. The MIA's original neoclassical building opened its doors in 1915 and the museum's permanent collection includes world-famous works that span 5,000 years and represent the diversity of the world's regions and cultures. More than 500,000 people visit the museum yearly, and the MIA, which has a major outreach program to elementary school kids, is the state's largest arts educator. You would think that it would cost big bucks to visit a stunning building filled with beautiful art, but you would be wrong: Admission to the museum is free. Every day. www.artsmia.org.

Weisman Art Museum. The Frederick R. Weisman Art Museum opened in 1934 as a teaching museum for the University of Minnesota. It features early twentieth century American artists, including Georgia O'Keeffe and Marsden Hartley, as well as such specialties as ceramics, Korean furniture, and ancient pottery of the American Southwest. The Weisman moved into new digs in 1993: a shiny, whimsical, stainless steel-and- brick building designed by architect Frank Gehry that perches on a bluff above the Mississippi River. The building is seen as the precursor to Gehry's Guggenheim Museum in Bilbao, Spain, which has a similar shimmery metallic undulating presence.

LITERATURE
Sinclair Lewis: Down on Main Street

There is no greater chronicler of the early 20th-century Midwest than Sinclair Lewis. The son of a country doctor, Lewis was born in 1885 in the central-Minnesota village of Sauk Centre.

Lewis had a keen eye and ear for the mores of the middle region of the country, and took on such topics as business, medicine, science, religion, and politics. Lewis's portrayal of Midwestern small towns and

They said it

"One of the most treasured American myths had been that all American villages were peculiarly noble and happy, and here an American attacked that myth. Scandalous. Some hundreds of thousands read the book with the same masochistic pleasure that one has in sucking an aching tooth."

— Sinclair Lewis describing reaction to his 1920 novel
Main Street in his lecture accepting the 1930 Nobel Prize

cities in such novels as *Main Street, Babbitt, Arrowsmith,* and *Elmer Gantry* is hardly flattering. American idealism and optimism are on display, but so too are conformism, boosterism, and empty striving after material wealth. *Main Street,* his best-known novel, is based on the Sauk Centre of his boyhood, and Lewis demonstrates a critical affection toward his hometown.

As a 17-year-old, Lewis left Minnesota for a year at Oberlin Academy, followed by study at Yale University. Thereafter, he led a peripatetic existence, traveling widely in the US and abroad, and living in a number of American locales, as well as in Europe, where he spent much of the last decade of his life. He died in Rome in 1951. Lewis, an alcoholic, did not have an easy life — one of his sons was killed in World War II, and he was twice divorced.

Lewis's best known works were produced during the 1920s, although he published a number of other books both before and after this period. He was awarded (and declined) the 1926 Pulitzer Prize for *Arrowsmith,* and in 1930 received the Nobel Prize for Literature. He accepted this latter award, and was the first American writer to receive the Nobel for Literature.

Sinclair Lewis is buried in Greenwood Cemetery in Sauk Centre. The Sinclair Lewis Boyhood Home, located on Sinclair Lewis Avenue, is open for tours. The house has been restored with period furnishings, including many items that belonged to the Lewis family themselves.

THE TALE OF DICAMILLO

Children's writer Kate DiCamillo moved from her native Florida to Minneapolis while in her 20s. She was homesick, found her first Minnesota winter hard-going, and pined for a dog (her apartment building didn't allow pets).

Rather than head home, DiCamillo, like so many newcomers to Minnesota, put her nose to the grindstone. The result? *Because of Winn-Dixie*, her smash debut novel. The story features a big dog who "adopts" a 10-year-old girl newly relocated to a small Florida town. The book, which was published in 2001, garnered a Newbery Honor and was subsequently made into a movie. Since then, DiCamillo, who still lives in Minneapolis, has written a number of other titles, including picture books, stories for young readers (starring Mercy Watson, the "porcine wonder"), and young adult novels, such as *The Tale of Despereaux, The Tiger Rising,* and *The Miraculous Journey of Edward Tulane.* In 2014 she was named "National Ambassador of Young People's Literature" by the Library of Congress.

MAYDAY

The long Minnesota winters are quickly forgotten on the first Sunday in May when a wild, colorful, unconventional parade comprising giant papier-mâché puppets, masked people on stilts, a marching band, and wagons and floats decorated with flowers and animals heads down Bloomington Avenue in Minneapolis toward Powderhorn Park.

The May Day Parade, organized by In the Heart of the Beast Puppet and Mask Theatre, culminates in the Tree of Life Ceremony in the park. The parade has been going since 1975 when 50 or so people (and some puppets,

Did you know. . .

that Prince wrote a fight song for the Minnesota Vikings prior to their playoff matchup with New Orleans Saints in January 2010? The lyrics to "Purple and Gold" include the words: "4ever strong as the wind that blows the Vikings' horn." The team loved the song, but unfortunately, the Vikes lost the game 31-28.

banners, and accordions) celebrated the end of the Vietnam War. This tradition of political and social engagement continues to this day.

The event is a community endeavor. Each year, public meetings are held starting in February to decide a theme for the festival and parade. Past themes have included water, the economy, war, and corn. Yes, corn.

Once the procession arrives at Powderhorn Lake, huge puppets representing the woods, river, sky, and prairie open the ceremony. The show ends as canoes carry a giant sun across the water to the sound of drumming and cheers from the masses. It's been described as a cross between a circus, a grand historical pageant, and an ancient ritual.

Weblinks

Explore Minnesota

www.exploreminnesota.com.

The state tourism site is a good resource for outdoor activities, shopping, theater, and more throughout the state.

Minnesota Monthly

www.minnesotamonthly.com.

A monthly publication emphasizing food, the arts, style, travel, and more.

Secrets of the City

www.secretsofthecity.com.

The "daily digest of Twin Cities culture" features events, openings, restaurants, and issues of interest.

Did you know. . .

that there are 20 casinos in Minnesota? Mystic Lake Casino Hotel, located in Prior Lake just south of Minneapolis, is the biggest with 4,000 slots, 100 table games, and a 2,100-seat auditorium. Another biggie is Grand Casino Hinckley, which has more than 2,000 slots and lies halfway between the Twin Cities and Duluth.

Food

Minnesota is a food lover's haven. Centuries before Minnesota was christened the Bread and Butter State at the 1902 Pan-American Exposition in Buffalo, NY, the original residents were already keyed in to the abundance of locally-grown food.

When the French voyageurs arrived in the late 1600s, they found the Dakota foraging wild strawberries, blueberries, blackberries, and walnuts. They grew corn, beans, and squash, harvested wild rice from the northern lakes, and netted and speared the fish that swam in those lakes. Today, fried walleye with wild rice, corn and beans, with blueberry pie for dessert, is an iconic Minnesota meal.

Minnesota's melting pot is filled with flavors added by each wave of immigrants. In the 1800s, Scandinavians, Germans, Czechs, Finns, and Italians moved in, bringing lutefisk, lefse, beer, sauerkraut, sausage, cardamom, borscht, garlic, and Roma tomatoes. Mexican migrant farm workers brought chilies, rice, and beans in the 1920s, and Southeast Asians refugees gave us their taste for hot, sour and bitter flavors as they began arriving in the 1980s. Now, spring rolls and Hmong fried rice are as commonplace on a Minnesota supper table as tuna noodle hotdish and a green-bean salad.

TAKE 5 FIVE ITEMS YOU CAN GET
"ON A STICK" AT THE MINNESOTA STATE FAIR

1. Alligator sausage
2. Chocolate-covered cheesecake
3. Deep-fried bacon with caramelized maple syrup
4. Tater-tot hotdish with cream of mushroom dipping sauce
5. Chocolate-covered watermelon

A MINNESOTA FOOD GLOSSARY

Beer batter: Flour, egg, and seasonings blended with beer to coat fish before frying.

Bison: North American buffalo, which once roamed the prairie, now raised for their meat at bison ranches in the state.

Boiled sausage: Usually served with sauerkraut or braised cabbage, with potatoes boiled with the sausage.

Crappies: Small fish that are easily caught in the spring. Several make a meal.

Deer sausage: A mixture of ground venison and various spices stuffed into casings.

Fiddlehead ferns: Edible pale green ferns shaped like the scroll of a violin; found in forests in May.

Did you know. . .

that three food advertising icons from Minnesota are on the top 10 list of ad icons at AdAge.com: the Pillsbury Doughboy, Green Giant, and Betty Crocker?

TAKE 5 JEREMY IGGERS' FIVE WAYS
MINNESOTANS' EATING
HABITS HAVE CHANGED

Jeremy Iggers is an award-winning journalist who wrote about food and restaurants for more than 20 years at the *Minneapolis Star Tribune*. He is now executive director of the Twin Cities Media Alliance, the nonprofit organization that operates the online newspaper *Twin Cities Daily Planet*.

1. **Minnesota diners have become more adventurous, and they have a lot more choices.** When I started writing about Minnesota restaurants in 1976, there was an almost complete lack of diversity in the local dining scene. There were a handful of ethnic restaurants in the Twin Cities: the Nankin, Howard Wong's, Fuji-ya, Vescio's, and Casa Coronado. Maybe one or two more. Now we have an incredible variety of ethnic cuisines, ranging from Vietnamese and Hmong, Korean, and Filipino to Ecuadorian, Russian, Ethiopian, and Somali.

2. **Minnesota diners are more sophisticated.** When I started reviewing, the most sophisticated restaurant in Minneapolis was called Charlie's Cafe Exceptionale. It was most famous for its potato salad and kitchen-sink sandwich. (They also did French dishes.)

3. **Minnesota diners are pickier.** The overall level of quality is much higher; bad restaurants just don't survive.

4. **Minnesota diners have become more ethnically aware.** If there is a defining Twin Cities cuisine these days, it is defined by the chefs at restaurants like Lucia's, Corner Table, Common Roots, Gardens of Salonica, Sea Change, etc., who build their values-driven menus around local (except for Sea Change), sustainable ingredients from small producers.

5. **One thing hasn't changed.** Minnesotans still love big portions.

1. **The Annual Rhubarb Festival** in Lanesboro
2. **Hopkins Raspberry Festival** in Hopkins
3. **Blueberry Festival** in Lake George
4. **Potato Days** in Barnesville
5. **King Turkey Day** in Worthington

Fish fry: A meal usually consisting of battered deep-fried fish, French fries, and cole-slaw. Popular during Lent, when Roman Catholics often abstain from eating meat products on Fridays.

Fry bread: A wheat flour dough deep-fried and sprinkled with sugar or salt, or topped with maple syrup; sold at tribal powwows or late-summer festivals.

Kolachke: Sweet buns claimed by the Czechs and Poles of the region. Usually filled with prunes, apricots, poppy seed, or cottage cheese.

Jucy Lucy: A hamburger stuffed with cheese, said to have originated at Matt's Bar in south Minneapolis. Many area restaurants serve variations, including the Blue Door Pub in St. Paul, which serves a Bangkok Blucy stuffed with mozzarella cheese soaked in coconut milk, and served with curry sauce for dunking.

They said it

"Recipes…were one of the few things immigrants could carry from the old world to the new world with ease. Tastes from home sustained those that tried to forge a new life in the wilds of Minnesota."
— Mollee Francisco, Oct. 15, 2009, *Chaska Herald*

Lefse: A traditional Scandinavian flatbread similar to a tortilla and made of mashed potatoes.

Lutefisk: A traditional Nordic dish made of dried whitefish soaked in lye that tends to be eaten by those of Norwegian lineage around the Christmas holiday.

Morel: A cone-shaped, sponge-like mushroom that comes up in the spring. Minnesota's state mushroom.

Pemmican: Dried meat and berries pounded with a stone and mixed with fat and marrow. The Objibwe packed the pemmican into hide sacks, sealing them with melted fat. It could keep for up to three years.

Pierogies: Dumplings filled with mashed potatoes, onions, cheese, or cabbage; boiled or fried, or both.

Shore lunch: A traditional meal on the shores of the lakes where fishermen cook their catch on an open fire. In the Boundary Waters Canoe Area, guides prepare the fish for their guests.

They said it

"Between Duluth and Grand Marais is probably the best eating/driving trip in the whole state. I'd start with lunch at the old-fashioned Pickwick steakhouse (Duluth), go to Russ Kendall's Smoke House (Knife River) for smoked fish, Satellite's Country Inn (Schroeder) for raisin pie, and World's Best Donut (Grand Marais) — they make a flat Scandinavian bread with cinnamon and sugar, which I don't think is made anywhere else. You have to stop at all the cozy, small-town cafes where pudgy grandmas still make wild rice and chicken soup from scratch, or the Lockport Grill (Lutsen), where they make apple fritters three times a day."

— **Andrew Zimmern, food writer, TV personality, chef and teacher**

Smörgåsbord: A Scandinavian meal served buffet-style with a variety of food, often served on Christmas Eve in Swedish homes.

Sugaring: Collecting maple sap from trees and boiling it down to make sugar.

TAKE 5

FIVE MINNESOTA ITEMS
ANDREW ZIMMERN MISSES WHEN HE'S ON THE ROAD

Andrew Zimmern is a food writer, TV personality, chef, and teacher who lives in Minneapolis. As the co-creator, host, and contributing producer of Travel Channel's hit series, *Bizarre Foods with Andrew Zimmern*, *Bizarre Foods America* and *Andrew Zimmern's Bizarre World*, he travels the world, exploring the food in its own territory. Zimmern is also a columnist at *Mpls.St.Paul Magazine* and his writing appears in numerous national publications including *Delta Sky Magazine* and *Bon Appétit*. He is the author of the books *The Bizarre Truth* and *Andrew Zimmern's Field Guide to Exceptionally Weird, Wild, and Wonderful Foods*. His website, andrewzimmern.com is a treasure trove of food and culture stories, podcasts, videos and recipes.

According to Andrew, "I'm on the road 35 to 37 weeks a year, and I choose Minnesota because it's not New York or L.A.. When I'm home, I'm not doing anything industry-related . . . if you do what I do for a living, and live in New York or L.A., you're on all the time. I'm away from my wife and son and dog and cat so much that I never want to leave my house."

1. **My wife's traditional Minnesota grandma–style cooking.** When I've been on the road for three weeks in Southeast Asia eating jungle rat, I can't wait for my wife's tater-tot-hotdish. I dream about her roasted chicken with lemon and rosemary on flights home.

Swedish meatballs: A mixture of ground beef, pork, veal, and spices, including cardamom, and traditionally served on the Christmas Eve smörgåsbord.

Tailgate: A casual social event held in stadium parking lots that involves grilling meat and drinking alcoholic beverages.

2. **I'm a Jew from New York City so comfort food falls into three categories for me:** Chinese food, pizza, and my grandmother's food. Punch Pizza is one of the five best pizza joints in the country.
3. **I think some of our Southeast Asian cuisine** can compete with restaurants in New York City, L.A., Toronto, Vancouver, and other traditional hotbeds of ethnic dining. People are really, really shocked.
4. **The St. Paul Farmers Market with my son.** Nothing helps me plug back in faster than wandering around, seeing the market through his eyes: Minnesota cheese makers and orchard owners and veggie growers and free-range chicken producers. We have some most radically fantastic farm-to-table food systems in Minnesota, blessedly undiluted by the cloying tug of commercialism. Every single day I'm in Minnesota in season, I go to Deardorff Orchards in Waconia. I'll go four or five days in a row. I adore getting on the truck, picking Honeycrisp and Zestar. They press fresh cider; it runs clear into our cup. It's extraordinary.
5. **I go to the State Fair every single day it runs.** We slow down and we do area by area. You gotta get the footlong hot dog across from the Giant Slide. The permanent fairgrounds that maintain 4-H roots is magic, and you can still get an amazing Gizmo Italian sandwich. Oh, and mini-cinnamon rolls, French fries, and cheese curds in the Food Building.

Walleye: The Minnesota state fish, called the "sole of freshwater fish" because it's so versatile.

TAKE 5 FIVE MINNESOTA CAFES
WHERE YOU CAN GET MORE
THAN JUST GOOD FOOD

1. **Al's Breakfast** in the Dinkytown neighborhood of Minneapolis may be the tiniest restaurant you'll ever eat in. The place is 10 feet wide and has just 14 stools at the counter that are always filled. Dining with a friend and a seat opens five people away from another open stool? Al's staff will politely rearrange the seating to accommodate you.

On weekends, it's a long wait to order a stack of blueberry pancakes, a bacon waffle, or those buttery hashbrowns, as there's usually a line of bleary-eyed co-eds snaking its way down 14th Avenue. Al's has been dishing up breakfast food in this University of Minnesota neighborhood for 60 years.

Its anniversary celebration in May 2010 featured performances by two brass bands (outside, of course) and the debut of a special suite written and performed by Prof. Lips, David Baldwin (professor of trumpet and co-ordinator of brass instruments at the university). The special that day was banana pancakes. Laurie Lindeen, former Zuzu's Petals singer-turned-author and wife to Replacements' Paul Westerberg, worked the counter there for a decade.

2. **The Angry Trout Café** in Grand Marais sits at a dock on Lake Superior. You can watch the fishing boats, the sometimes-giant waves, and the seagulls while you eat fresh Lake Superior fish, locally-grown produce, and hand-harvested wild rice mixed with cranberries.

The food is served on handmade pottery, and the pint-size cloth napkins are hand-sewn. It's only open from May through mid-October, and not only does it have great food (we recommend the whitefish chowder, fish fritters, smoked herring, smoked trout fettuccine, and the ginger-lime vinaigrette), it's got a very cool rest-room. It's a small building just outside the front door of the café with its own heating system and some gorgeous tile work.

Wild rice: A staple food for Minnesota's native tribes for centuries. Now the state grain. It's actually not rice but an aquatic grass whose seeds mature into dark brown kernels in late summer.

3. **The Corral Supper Club & Lounge** in Nelson is known for its tasty ribs, but its real attraction is "Shoot the Minnow," a gimmick where customers slam down five bucks to have a minnow placed in their shot glass (your choice of liquor) and then drink the shot, minnow in tow. The prize for swallowing the fish bait is a T-shirt that says, "I shot the minnow at the Corral." The folks in western Minnesota seem to like it: The café goes through thousands of shirts (and minnows) every year.

4. **Gordy's Hi Hat** in Cloquet marked 50 years serving hand-patted burgers, house-made onion rings, and hand-dipped battered fish in 2010. Each spring, owners Gordy and Marilyn Lundquist return from their winter home in Sarasota, FLA, to open the seasonal diner.

In May, Gordy's hits off the cruise season by holding a "Blessing of the Cars" in the parking lot. Gordy's is known for its food, but another attraction is Gordy himself. He still works the counter. Gordy's is a frequent stop for travelers heading up to the Boundary Waters Canoe Area.

5. **Mickey's Diner** in downtown St. Paul never sleeps. It's been open 24 hours a day 365 days a year for nearly 70 years, serving hashbrowns shredded from real potatoes, pancakes made from scratch, and eggs fried in butter. Real butter.

The art deco diner was designed to look like a railroad car and was purchased from the Jerry O'Mahoney Co. in New Jersey and shipped to Minnesota in 1940. It's been at 36 W. Seventh St. ever since. Mickey's is known for its ambience as much as its star status. Part of its character is molded by the fact that it's open all night long. You can also see it in all three *Mighty Ducks* movies, as well as in *Jingle All the Way*, and *A Prairie Home Companion*. Mickey's was placed on the National Register of Historic Places in 1983.

1. **Winter-hardy alfalfa:** farmer Wendelin Grimm, 1859
2. **Handled grocery bag:** St. Paul grocer Walter Deubener, 1912
3. **Pop-up toaster:** Stillwater mechanic Charles Strite, 1919
4. **Milky Way candy bar:** candy maker Frank C. Mars, 1923
5. **Crisp-crust frozen pizza:** restaurateur Rose Totino, 1979

TASTES CHANGE

Minnesotans eat more than hotdish, Jell-O, and recipes from the Lutheran church ladies' cookbook. Take a walk through a farmers market today and you'll see just how ethnically diverse this state is. Lemongrass, cilantro, and baby bok choy grown by Hmong farmers are stacked up next to booths selling free-range meats, smoked fish and goat cheese — all products grown, made and produced in Minnesota.

COMMUNITY-SUPPORTED AGRICULTURE

Minnesota ranks seventh in the nation in number of organic farms, according to a USDA survey. (California was first and Wisconsin second). According to the Minnesota Department of Agriculture, there are roughly 700 certified organic farms in the state. Since the 1990s, small organic vegetable farms have found their niche in community-supported agriculture (CSA). CSA provides a direct link between local farmers and consumers. Each season, members purchase a share of a farmer's crop before it is planted, which allows the farmer to pay for seed, water, and equipment up front and be less reliant on banks and loans. Beginning in June and running through October, each week the farmer delivers food to designated pick-up spots in the city. CSA membership is growing in the Twin Cities where people often have little space to farm large garden plots themselves. In 1990, there were two CSAs serving the Twin Cities metropolitan area; now there are dozens, and the Twin Cities CSA Farm Directory published by the Land Stewardship Project runs to 44 pages.

MOOSE & SQUIRREL

In 1866, Cadwallader C. Washburn built his first flour mill near the falls of St. Anthony on the Mississippi River in Minneapolis. Within 10 years he had built a second mill, and in 1877, John Crosby joined Washburn as a partner in the Washburn Crosby Co. In the late 1800s the company named its finest flour Gold Medal.

Charles Pillsbury started his milling company across the river from Washburn's facility during this time. In 1928, the two companies

A Saturday Tradition

The St. Paul Farmers Market was founded in 1853 and has grown considerably since then. It now represents the gold-standard for such enterprises, and has become a destination in its own right, a place to see and be seen. The products of the 170-plus vendors, and especially the vendors themselves, are discussed by Twin City foodies the way movie stars are dissected on *Entertainment Tonight*. All produce must be grown within a 50-mile radius of the market, and all other food must hail from Minnesota or western Wisconsin.

There is something magical and uplifting about arriving early at the Saturday-morning market. Urbanites delight in talking directly to farm folk, and in many instances they know each other by first names. The music of live bands fills the air, while shoppers nod to each other as they sip lattes and browse the aisles, perusing everything from apples, sugar snap peas, strawberries, kettle corn, zucchini, cheeses and fresh flowers, to organic baby food, vines, fresh herbs, candles, chocolates, and melons to maple syrup baked goods, poultry, buffalo, venison, beef, pork, lamb, eggs, plants and shrubs—you name it. On a peak Saturday, there could be as many as 30,000 people at the market. It has gotten to the point that shuttle buses have been added to take people to the mix. Today's Lowertown location at the corner of Fifth Street and Wall Street is near one of the market's original sites of over 150 years ago. For many years, the market was at Tenth and Jackson, but freeway construction forced the move to the current space in 1982.

merged and became General Mills. Under the leadership of James Ford Bell, the company created many well-known products that are still sold today, including Cheerios (originally coined Cheerioats), Kix, Bisquick, and Wheaties.

From the mid-1950s through the 1970s, General Mills sponsored many well-known television shows, including *Rocky and Bullwinkle Show*, featuring Rocket J. Squirrel and his sidekick, Bullwinkle J. Moose. When it debuted in 1959, audiences watched the moose and squirrel soar toward earth on a return visit from the moon. The two Frostbite Falls, residents had been blasted into outer space when the quick-rising mooseberry cake they were baking exploded. Subtle allusions to General Mills were often woven into the show's plots. In one episode, evil villain Boris Badenov tried to counterfeit cereal-box tops, saying they were "the real basis for the world's monetary system."

LOVELY SPAM! WONDERFUL SPAM!

More than 122 million cans of SPAM are sold throughout the world each year. (The biggest customer? Hawaii.) SPAM debuted in 1937, after Hormel Foods of Austin devised a recipe for a 12-ounce can of luncheon meat. Hormel produces much more than SPAM, but the little can of pork products gets most of the attention. There's even a SPAM Museum, a 16,000-sq-ft building filled with SPAM artifacts and all kinds of SPAM trinkets you can bring home to the relatives: SPAM Frisbees, SPAM beach balls, SPAM neckties, and, of course, SPAM cookbooks. And did we say admission is free?

The museum takes you through the product's role in feeding the troops during World War II up to Monty Python's *SPAMALOT*, a Broadway musical that debuted in 2005. When *SPAMALOT* premiered, the company released a special tin of SPAM.

The company kept a sense of humor when the British comedy troupe Monty Python immortalized SPAM with a 1970 comedy sketch. The three-and-a-half-minute skit takes place in a restaurant that serves SPAM with every menu item and includes a chorus of Vikings in horned

TAKE5 FIVE BLUE RIBBON RECIPES
FROM THE MINNESOTA STATE FAIR

These recipes were all first-place winners at the 2009 fair.

1. **Liam's SPAM Summer Salad:** a can of SPAM oven-roasted turkey, salad mix, ramen noodles (without the seasoning), bean sprouts, with a dressing made of rice vinegar, soy sauce, ginger, garlic, sugar, and oil. Great American SPAM Championship; Kid Chef Liam Anderson of St. Paul.

2. **Cherry Almond Energy Bars:** dates, honey, brown sugar, chunky almond butter, orange juice, dried cherries, raisins, mixed fruit bits, pepitas, cinnamon, Malt-O-Meal Honey & Oat Blenders with Almonds. Make it With Malt-O-Meal Recipe Contest; Danielle Gordanier of St. Paul.

3. **King's Chocolate 'n Caramel Cappuccino Cake:** King Arthur cake flour, sugar, baking soda, salt, baking powder, strong coffee, buttermilk, shortening, eggs, caramel extract, unsweetened chocolate. The caramel cheesecake layer is made with cream cheese, sugar, eggs, sour cream, coffee, and caramel extract. The frosting is made with butter, chocolate, sugar, and vanilla. King Arthur Flour Great Cake Contest; Renee Janas-Johnson of Brooklyn Park.

4. **Almond Joy Coffee Cake:** flour, yeast, milk, butter, sugar, salt, salt, and an egg. In the filling: butter, sugar, almond paste, egg white, almond extract, and in the glaze,: milk, almond extract, sugar, and a garnish of slivered almonds. Fleischmann's Yeast Best Ever Baking Contest; Martha DeHaven of Lino Lakes.

5. **Blueberry Heaven Pie:** Pillsbury refrigerated pie crusts, egg white, sugar for the crust; cream cheese, sugar, vanilla, and whipped topping for the cream layer; and blueberries, lemon juice, butter, sugar, salt, gelatin, cornstarch, lemon peel, and water for the fruit filling. Pillsbury Refrigerated Pie Crust Championship; Elaine Janas of Columbia Heights.

helmets who sing "SPAM, SPAM, SPAM, SPAM, lovely SPAM! Wonderful SPAM!" every time the word SPAM is spoken. Some say the sketch was a response to how the Brits felt about the product: It was one of the few meats that were not rationed in England during World War II.

Incidentally, Monty Python member and filmmaker Terry Gilliam was born in Medicine Lake, Minnesota.

BETTY CROCKER'S ORIGINS

Betty Crocker was born in 1921 after a highly successful Gold Medal flour promotion inundated the Washburn Crosby Co. of Minneapolis with customers' questions about baking. The company created the "Betty Crocker" pen name to personalize its responses to those queries. Betty rapidly became a multimedia superstar.

The company sponsored cooking schools across the country and even a radio show in 1924 —*The Betty Crocker Cooking School of the Air*—that quickly went national. Betty's face first appeared in 1937 as a portrait printed on the Softasilk cake-flour box. By 1945, Betty had become such a celebrity that she was voted the second-most-famous woman in America that year (Eleanor Roosevelt was No. 1), according to *Fortune*. Betty made numerous appearances on CBS and NBC, where she taught such stars as George Burns and Gracie Allen how to cook. She got her own show, *The Betty Crocker Search for the All-American Homemaker of Tomorrow*, in 1954.

For the next 21 years, a variety of actresses played Betty, while behind-the-scenes "Bettys" cranked out cookbooks. Since the 1950s, there have been more than 200 Betty Crocker cookbooks published.

BREWERIES

Head across the Hennepin Avenue Bridge in Minneapolis toward the northeast section of the city and you'll see a giant neon Grain Belt Beer sign looming over the Mississippi River, near the former bottling plant. Grain Belt has been brewed in Minnesota since 1893, first by the Minneapolis Brewing Co. and now Schell Brewery in New Ulm.

Minnesota has brewed some high-profile beers, including Hamm's. In the mid-20th century, the Hamm's bear and his woodland friends romped through the Land of Sky Blue Waters and put Minnesota on TV screens across the nation. These days, consumer taste has turned toward craft beer and there are plenty of small brewers in the state, including Summit Brewing of St. Paul, Surly of Brooklyn Center, and Brau Brothers of Lucan. Cold Spring Brewery in Cold Spring has been around for more than a century; it specializes in craft beer.

ANNUAL PER-CAPITA BEER CONSUMPTION

- Virginia: 29 gallons
- North Carolina: 29.1 gallons
- **Minnesota: 29.5 gallons**
- Oklahoma: 29.9 gallons
- Illinois: 31.3 gallons
- Vermont: 31.4 gallons
- Most beer consumed: Montana 43.5 gallons
- Least beer consumed: Utah 20.5 gallons
- U.S. average: 30.4 gallons

Source: Beer Institute Research; population figures are for individuals over 21 years of age

Economy

Home to 19 Fortune 500 companies, Minnesota is less reliant on a single industry—be it agriculture or manufacturing—than its neighbors, and the Twin Cities are a destination for bright and ambitious young people from across the region.

The average American home, from the breakfast table to the bedroom, living room, and office is chock-full of Minnesota-based products and brands. No U.S. kitchen is without food produced by Minnesota's own Cargill, General Mills, Land O'Lakes, or Hormel, and those goodies were likely purchased from one of many supermarket chains nationwide under the Supervalu umbrella. Target is one of America's top purveyors of clothes and household goods, and Best Buy is the nation's leading electronic goods retailer. The house itself? Think Andersen doors and windows, and 3M construction materials. As for the people inside, no, Minnesota is not in the cloning field, but UnitedHealth Group is one of the country's largest health insurers, the Mayo Clinic a premier health care and research facility, and Medtronic a global leader in the production of medical devices.

Agriculture, forestry, and mining have traditionally been the state's key industries and still rank as major sources of exports. Despite the importance of these areas, health care and education are the state's largest employers, and specialized manufacturing, retail trade, and the service sector are also major sources of jobs.

The Great Recession took its toll on the state and resulted in nearly a quarter of a million jobs lost, many of them in manufacturing, construction, and transportation. Minnesota counted more than 20,000 bankruptcies and over 23,000 home foreclosures in 2009 alone. Moreover, the state, like many others, had trouble paying its bills, and billions of dollars of cuts were made to balance the state budget. Notwithstanding these gloomy numbers, Minnesota's unemployment rate remained below the national average, and never reached the 9% recorded in the recession of 1982. Moreover, Minnesota came out of the recession in better shape than most states, and by 2013 had recovered the jobs lost in the downturn. Still, there is a sizeable number of people unemployed in the state, and wage growth has been near non-existent.

Did you know. . .

that Minnesota's first bank was the First National Bank of St. Paul? It was organized by Parker Paine in 1863 and was originally a private bank.

TAKE5 BEST PAID CEOS
AT PUBLICLY TRADED COMPANIES

(figures include salary, bonuses and stock options)

1. **Brian Cornell:** $28.16 million (Target)
2. **Jim Cracchiolo:** $24.46 million (Ameriprise Financial)
3. **Inge Thulin:** $20.12 million (3M)
4. **Douglas Baker Jr.:** $15.46 million (Ecolab)
5. **Richard Davis:** $11.18 million (U.S. Bancorp)

Source: *Minneapolis/St. Paul Business Journal*

GROSS DOMESTIC PRODUCT (GDP)

GDP represents the total value of goods and services produced.

- Minnesota: $294.73 billion
- U.S. GDP: $15,684.8 billion
- Minnesota's share of U.S. GDP: 1.88%
- Minnesota's share of the U.S. population: 1.71%
- Minnesota GDP per capita: $47,028
- U.S. GDP per capita: $42,784
- Minnesota's per capita rank nationally: 11

Sources: Latest available figures from the US Department of Commerce, Bureau of Economic Analysis; US Census Bureau; and Minnesota Department of Employment and Economic Development (DEED).

Did you know. . .

that 3M's full name is the Minnesota Mining and Manufacturing Co.? Founded in the Lake Superior town of Two Harbors in 1902, the company moved to Maplewood (where it is currently headquartered) in 1910. 3M, which makes a range of consumer, transportation, medical, electronics, and industrial products, records annual sales of $25.3 billion and is one of 30 companies comprising the Dow Jones Industrial Average. 3M has more than 75,000 employees worldwide and operates in 65 countries.

LEADING INDUSTRIES

Sector, number of jobs, and weekly wage:

- Education and health services: 676,654 ($893)
- Trade, transportation, and utilities: 523,909 ($806)
- Manufacturing: 307,300 ($1,089)
- Professional and business services: 346,720 ($1,259)
- Leisure and hospitality: 269,902 ($341)

On Target

The Target bull's eye ranks with the McDonald's "M" and the Nike "swoosh" in the pantheon of great trademarks. But Target is more than a famous logo — the Minneapolis-headquartered chain is a retail juggernaut, operating 1,740 stores in 49 states (Vermont is the lone holdout).

Despite a 2013 security breach which spooked shoppers and investors, and a costly and failed Canadian expansion which was ended in 2015, Target remains a retail giant. It rings up more than $72 billion in annual sales, and employs 350,000 people nationwide. It always ranks on *Fortune Magazine*'s "Most Admired Companies" list, and the Target Foundation gives back 5% of pretax profits to the community, a practice that began in the 1940s.

Target's direct ancestor is the Dayton Dry Goods Company, later known as Dayton's Department Store. Dayton's was founded in 1902 by New Yorker George D. Dayton on Nicollet Avenue in Minneapolis.

Dayton's was a typical mid-century regional department store chain, but it foresaw the possibilities of the post-war American suburb. In the 1950s, Dayton's was a key player in the establishment of the Southdale Mall in the Minneapolis suburb of Edina, the first fully enclosed shopping center in the nation.

In 1960, Dayton's took the bold step of establishing a discount chain to complement its department-store base. The

- Public administration: 123,868 ($972)
- Financial activities: 179,818 ($1,394)
- Construction: 107,426 ($1,054)
- Other services: 85,771 ($545)
- Information: 57,036 ($1,199)
- Natural resources and mining: 27,575 ($796)

Source: Latest available data from DEED, Occupational Employment Statistics (OES) Wage Data

famous bull's eye logo debuted in 1962, when Target opened its first store in Roseville. Four years later, Denver was the site of the first Target store outside of Minnesota.

In its early years, Target was merely one piece of the Dayton Corp. (later Dayton-Hudson after its merger with Detroit retailer J.L. Hudson), but by the mid-1970s, Target was the company's biggest revenue producer. In the late 1980s, Target was operating stores in every region of the country, and in 2000 the Dayton Hudson Corp. was renamed Target Corp., a reflection of Target's dominance. Target's parent, Dayton, no longer exists — it was subsumed under the Marshall Field's brand in 2001 and sold in 2004.

Long a place to stock up on socks, or purchase a laundry bin or toaster, Target woos middle-class consumers with affordable yet attractive goods. Target differentiates itself from the "Marts" (K and Wal) by its emphasis on style. To be sure, Target is a discounter appealing to mainstream America, but it has hired young designers to craft its clothing lines, and in everything from household goods to junior fashions tries to project a contemporary and fun look. As such, Target has become the default store for many: inexpensive enough to satisfy the budget-conscious, but sufficiently upscale to appeal to those who blanch at dollar stores.

CLASSES OF WORKER

- Private wage and salary workers   80.4%
- Government workers   12.4%
- Self-employed in own unincorporated business   6.9%
- Unpaid family workers   0.3%

GENERATIONAL WORKFORCE

Total Minnesota workforce: 2,659,297

Age bracket	Employees	Percentage of total
14-18	107,546	4.0
19-21	147,691	5.5
22-24	179,132	6.7
25-34	576,069	21.7
35-44	583,977	22.0
45-54	625,396	23.5
65-99	89,984	3.4

Source: LEHD State of Minnesota WIA Reports — Quarterly Workforce Indicators

TAKE5 FIVE MINNESOTA BILLIONAIRES

1. **Whitney MacMillan**. $4.4 billion; Cargill heir (Minneapolis).
2. **Stanley Hubbard**. $2.1 billion; DirecTV (St. Paul).
3. **Glen Taylor**. $1.9 billion; founder of printing and communications company the Taylor Corp. (Mankato).
4. **Marilyn Carlson Nelson & family**. $ 1.1 billion; heir and former CEO of the Carlson Cos (Long Lake).
5. **Barbara Carlson Gage & family**. $1.1 billion; heir to the Carlson Cos and head of the family foundation (Long Lake)

Source: *Forbes Magazine*

PERSONAL INCOME

Minnesota ranks 13th in the nation with a per-capita personal income of $48, 998. The U.S. figure is $46,049. Minnesota outstrips neighboring states in per-capita income with the exception of North Dakota, which has experienced an energy boom in recent years. Per capita income represents total state income divided by residents, and does not account for taxes or for income distribution.

PER CAPITA INCOME FOR MINNESOTA'S NEIGHBORS

- Wisconsin: $44,186
- Iowa: $44,937
- North Dakota: $55,802
- South Dakota: $45,279
- Nebraska: $47,557

Source: U.S. Department of Commerce, Bureau of Economic Analysis

HOUSEHOLD INCOME

Median household income for Minnesota and its neighbors

- Minnesota: $67,244
- Wisconsin: $58,050
- Nebraska: $56,870
- Iowa: $57,810
- South Dakota: $53,053
- North Dakota: $60,730

Did you know. . .

that the Mall of America attracts more annual visitors than Disney Land, Disney World, and the Grand Canyon combined?

GENDER (IM)BALANCE

Women have made dramatic progress in educational attainment in the past four decades, but these gains have yet to translate into equity in pay—even for college-educated women who work full-time. Female earnings in the U.S. represent approximately 76.5% of male earnings. In Minnesota, the figure is almost 80 percent, with women earning an average of $40,595 and men $50,885. Minnesota ranks 17th in the country in pay equity, and is better in this respect that its neighbors Wisconsin, the Dakotas and Iowa. Nationwide, Maryland and Nevada have the greatest parity with women earning roughly 85 percent of men's wages, while Wyoming brings up the rear at 64 percent.

TAKE5 FIVE MINNESOTA
INVENTIONS

1. **Post-it Notes.** The ubiquitous Post-it was launched nationwide by St. Paul's 3M in 1980.

2. **Tonka trucks.** The Tonka Corp., named after Lake Minnetonka and now part of the Rhode Island-based toymaker Hasbro, developed the sturdy trucks in the late 1940s.

3. **The Pacemaker.** The first battery-powered external pacemaker began ticking in the late 1950s. It was developed by Medtronic of Firdley.

4. **Rollerblades.** In 1979 hockey-playing brothers Scott and Brennan Olsen found an antique pair of roller skates in a Minneapolis store and use them to invent a new kind of roller skate. Rollerblades, the company, was founded in 1983.

5. **The pop-up toaster.** In 1919, Charles Strite, a mechanic at a plant in Stillwater, invented the pop-up toaster. The device was patented in 1921, and such toasters became particularly popular with the advent of sliced bread in the late 1920s.

Did you know...

that among Minnesota cities with a population greater than 5,000, Orono has the highest per capita income at $65,825 per person? The city of nearly 8,000 lies 25 miles west of Minneapolis.

Did you know...

that the strongest job growth in Minnesota in this century has been in the northwest suburbs of the Twin Cities? Not all is sunny in the metro area, however, as both Ramsey County and Hennepin County have lost jobs during this period.

MINNESOTA STATE TAXES

Total state and local taxes paid: $ 30 billion

- Individual income tax: 31.6% of total
- Sales and use tax: 21.2% (the sales tax rate is 6.875%)
- Property tax : 28.5%
- Corporate tax: 4.3%
- Other taxes: 14.2 %(includes motor vehicle registration tax, cigarette taxes and fees, insurance premiums taxes, MinnesotaCare taxes)

Source: Minnesota Department of Revenue.

They said it

"The worst of the recession is over, we are in the recovery, but it's slow. It's going to be one of the slowest recoveries we've had, maybe since the Great Depression."

— Tony Barrett, Ph.D., economics professor at The College of St. Scholastica in Duluth, in an early 2010 interview on Minnesota Public Radio

Minnesota has four tax brackets

Rates for a single person:

5.35% (less than $24,680)

7.05% ($24,681 to $81,080)

7.85% ($81,081 to $152,540)

9.85% (above $152,541)

The Malling of America

Visitors may appreciate Minnesota's natural wonders and cultural riches, but they beeline for Bloomington's 4.2-million-square-foot Mall of America. Big enough to accommodate seven Yankee Stadiums, the mall is the nation's largest and is home to more than 500 stores and 50 restaurants. The MoA chalks up 40 million visitors yearly (40% of them tourists) and generates $2 billion in economic activity.

Known locally as "the Megamall," MoA opened in 1992 at a cost of $650 million, (nearly $1.5 billion in today's dollars). Canada's Ghermezian Brothers, fresh off the opening of North America's other mall behemoth—the West Edmonton Mall in Alberta—saw opportunity locally and jumped on it. The draw was a vacant 100-acre parcel (once home to Met Stadium where the Twins and Vikings played) in the center of the Twin Cities metropolitan region. Combine Minnesota's peculiar love affair with malls—and its brutal winters, which make shopping in a climate controlled environment appealing—and you have a winner.

At its center is the 30-ride, 7-acre Nickelodeon Universe theme park. Mall thrill-seekers can also visit a speedway and a flight simulator, and those in the mood for love (or marriage, anyway) can get hitched at the Chapel of Love, which has conducted 5,000 ceremonies since its opening. The Mall of America concept is to unite shopping, entertainment, leisure, and even community, under one roof.

It's no shocker that Minnesota is home to the country's biggest mall, as it is also the site of the first fully enclosed such

They said it

"If you put fences around people, you get sheep. Give people the room they need."
— William L. McKnight, McKnight Foundation founder and former 3M CEO

venue in the U.S. The Southdale Center lies less than seven miles west of the Mall of America in Edina. The money to build the mall, which opened in 1956, came from the Dayton Co. (which eventually became Target). The vision for the mall, however, belonged to Victor Gruen, an Austrian-born architect who saw malls as the antidote to urban sprawl, a kind of town square for the new suburban landscape.

It was Gruen's idea to enclose the shopping center under a single roof, array stores along two levels instead of one, and incorporate a "garden court" (an atrium with a skylight that allowed natural light). Southdale, which included these features and the familiar department-store "anchor" tenants, would serve as a virtual blueprint for the hundreds of malls built across the country in the succeeding decades. Though malls would later be blamed for killing downtown shopping districts, Southdale was heralded by the most progressive architects of the age, including Frank Lloyd Wright.

Southdale still exists, and the Twin Cities are ringed by the Dale mall siblings: Rosedale (Roseville), Ridgedale (Minnetonka), and now shuttered Brookdale, reborn as Shingle Creek Crossing. The Mall of America is the unquestioned Big Daddy, and has replaced Paul Bunyan as the state's best-known colossus. It's Gruen's original utopian vision taken to its logical extreme; a city unto itself with a downtown's worth of stores, restaurants, and attractions, and 11,000 year-round employees. And it's not finished yet, the Mall's "Phase II Expansion" is projected to add another five million square-feet of space including a water park, hotels and offices.

TAKE5 FIVE LARGEST
NONPROFITS

1. **Blue Cross & Blue Shield, Eagan:** $9.5 billion (yearly revenues)
2. **Mayo Clinic, Rochester:** $9.3 billion
3. **Medica, Minnetonka:** $ 4.6 billion
4. **HealthPartners, Bloomington:** $ 4.0 billion
5. **Allina Health System, Minneapolis:** $3.4 billion

Source: *Minneapolis Star Tribune*

TAX FREEDOM DAY

Tax freedom day is the date on which earnings no longer go to taxes. It's calculated by dividing total taxes collected by total income. Selected "Freedom Days" are listed below.

- Louisiana and Mississippi: March 29 (earliest in nation)
- South Dakota: April 4
- Iowa: April 9
- North Dakota: April 18
- Wisconsin: April 20
- Minnesota: April 23 (seventh-latest, between California and Oregon)
- Connecticut: May 13 (latest in the nation)

Source: Tax Foundation

Did you know. . .

that according to the National Science Foundation, the Twin Cities metro area ranks sixth in the nation (between Chicago and San Diego) in R&D spending nationwide? Major Minnesota investors in R&D activities include 3M, General Mills, Medtronic and St. Jude Medical.

TAKE5 ERIC WIEFFERING'S FIVE KEYS
TO MINNESOTA AND THE FORTUNE 500

St. Paul resident Eric Wieffering is a former business columnist at the Minneapolis *Star Tribune*, and now supervises coverage of local and regional news, including politics, education, and the environment.

1. **Deep roots.** 3M Co. (ranked number 106), General Mills (155), and Hormel Foods (340) are almost as old as the state itself and reflect Minnesota's mining and agricultural roots. But they've evolved with the times. General Mills may have begun life as a grain processor, but today it houses some of the world's best-known consumer brands, including Wheaties cereal and Yoplait yogurt. At Hormel in Austin they still slaughter hogs, but SPAM and Jennie-O Turkey are carried in grocery stores across the country. 3M is one of the most diversified manufacturing companies in the world (although Scotch Tape and the Post-it are its most famous products).

2. **New kids on the block.** The nation's largest independent electronics retailer, Best Buy was founded in 1966 and UnitedHealth Group, one of the nation's largest managed-care companies, was formed in 1977.

3. **Mergers.** Great Minnesota companies have disappeared over the years, usually as a result of mergers. Most recently, Northwest Airlines was acquired by Atlanta-based Delta Air Lines and Travelers Cos., which came to Minnesota via acquisition of The St. Paul Cos., relocated to the East Coast. Pillsbury was sold to a British conglomerate in the 1980s before being sold again to General Mills in 2000.

4. **Gone.** Electronics manufacturer Honeywell, 73rd on the 2010 list, relocated to New Jersey after Allied-Signal bought it and kept the name. Control Data Corp., a mainstay of the mainframe computer industry, was 76th on the 1984 Fortune 500, but stumbled as the world shifted to personal computers.

5. **Missing.** *Fortune* ranks publicly traded companies, so some very large—but privately held—Minnesota firms do not appear. Case in point: Wayzata-based Cargill Inc. Cargill is Minnesota's largest company, and the largest privately held company in the U.S.

1. **Carver** (25)
2. **Scott** (36)
3. **Dakota** (73)
4. **Wright** (90)
5. **Sherburne** (98)

Source: *Washington Post*

IF THE TRAIN'S ON TIME . . .

Minnesotans' mean travel time to work is 21.9 minutes; in the Minneapolis-St. Paul-Bloomington metropolitan statistical area, the commute averages 23.9 minutes. And how do people get to work?

Mode	Minnesota	Twin Cities
Driving alone in car/truck/van:	77%	79%
Carpooling in car/truck/van:	10.4%	8.8%
Public transportation (including taxis):	3.2%	4.1%
Walk:	3.3%	2.4%
Other means:	0.9%	1.5%
Work at home:	4.6%	4.5%

Source: US Census Bureau

Did you know. . .

that in 1987 Minnesota became the first state to require employers to offer parental leave to both the mother and father of a newborn child?

TAKE5 FIVE MOST EXPENSIVE CITIES
IN WHICH TO BUY A HOUSE

Median value of a single-family home.

1. Spring Park
2. Deephaven
3. Orono
4. Wayzata
5. Tonka Bay

Source: Most recent figures available from NeighborhoodScout

HOME, SWEET HOME

Over 71% of Minnesotans own their own homes, which is slightly less than was the case in the mid-2000s. Like almost everywhere in the U.S., since the turn of the millennium there has been a rollercoaster ride in home prices. Prices in the 13-county Twin Cities metro area peaked in June 2006 with a median selling price of $237,000. They dropped as low as $150,000 in early 2009. Since that time, there has been an uneven recovery, with some cities posting record gains in home appreciation, while others languish well below boom-time highs. Median house prices:

- Minnesota: $183,000 (US: $182,800)
- Minneapolis: $203,500
- St. Paul: $168,200
- Rochester (metro): $166,300
- Duluth: $127,700
- Bloomington: $212,600

Source: Latest available figures from Zillow.com and *Forbes*

Did you know. . .

that *Fortune* magazine's list of the 100 Best Companies to work for in the U.S. includes General Mills, based in Golden Valley, and Rochester's Mayo Clinic?

TAKE5 FIVE INEXPENSIVE CITIES
IN WHICH TO BUY A HOUSE

1. **Dumont**
2. **Williams**
3. **Lancaster**
4. **Motley**
5. **Lamberton**

MONTHLY HOMEOWNERSHIP COSTS
- Minnesota: $1,044
- Iowa: $829
- Michigan: $972
- North Dakota: $818
- South Dakota: $828
- Wisconsin: $1,024

RENTING
Median rents for a two-bed room apartment
- Minnesota: $1,150 (US $1,080)
- St. Anthony: $1,500
- Minneapolis: $1,350
- St. Paul: $1,020

Source: Apartment List

Did you know. . .

that 24% of all tourism expenditures by visitors to the state occur in winter?

FORTUNE 500

Minnesota is overrepresented relative to its population on the Fortune 500, and is home to 18 such firms. The following are the Minnesota companies appearing on the most recent Fortune 500 list:

- UnitedHealth Group Inc., health insurance and services
- Target Corp., retailer
- Best Buy Co., electronics retailer
- CHS Inc., energy and agricultural cooperative
- Supervalu Inc., food retailer/wholesaler
- 3M Co., diversified manufacturer
- U.S. Bancorp, bank
- General Mills Inc., food manufacturer
- Medtronic Inc., medical devices
- Land O'Lakes Inc., farmer-owned dairy cooperative
- Ecolab Inc., cleaning products
- C.H. Robinson Worldwide Inc., transportation logistics and food sourcing
- The Mosaic Co., fertilizer maker
- Ameriprise Financial, financial services
- Xcel Energy Inc., utility
- Hormel Foods Corp., food manufacturer
- Thrivent Financial for Lutherans, financial planning
- St. Jude Medical, medical devices

Did you know. . .

that Christensen Farms in Brown County is the largest family-owned swine producer in the world and one of the top three producers in the U.S.? It raises 3 million pigs yearly.

TAKE 5 FIVE MINNESOTA
INDUSTRIAL TITANS

1. **Earl E. Bakken (1924 –).** Engineer, philanthropist and co-founder of Medtronic Inc., Bakken is the brain behind numerous life-altering medical devices, including the first battery-operated pacemaker. Bakken was fascinated with electricity as a boy, and even made his own electroshock device to ward off bullies. The Bakken Museum is "a one-of-a-kind museum exploring the mysteries of our electric world" is located in South Minneapolis.

2. **William Norris (1911–2006).** Norris had many entrepreneurial years under his belt before the 1957 birth of Control Data Corp., creator of the world's fastest computers. CDC's 6600, which out-performed everything on the market by tenfold, infuriated IBM because its staff of thousands could not keep pace with CDC's staff of 34. IBM retaliated by announcing the fictional release of Model 92. The nonexistent computer killed 6600 sales, prompting Norris to file and win a $600 million antitrust suit against IBM. Norris, also respected for his social activism, used CDC's expansion in the late 1960s to bring jobs to inner cities and disadvantaged communities. The company no longer exists, the result of a series of sales, spinoffs, and buyouts in the 1980s and '90s.

3. **William L. McKnight (1887–1978).** Despite his not having fully completed training, Minnesota Mining and Manufacturing Co. (3M) hired McKnight in 1907 as an assistant bookkeeper. He quickly rose through the ranks, becoming president in 1929 and chairman of the board in 1949. McKnight's greatest contribution was creating a corporate culture that encouraged employee autonomy, initiative, and innovation.

4. **Curt Carlson (1914–2006).** "Ultra-entrepreneur" Carlson founded the Gold Bond Stamp Co. in 1938 with a $55 loan. During the Great Depression, Carlson used Gold Bond Stamps to create consumer incentives for grocery stores. In 1973, the company was renamed Carlson Cos. and began diversifying into the hospitality and travel industries. Carlson Cos. remains a prominent player in this area, fielding such brands as Radisson, T.G.I. Friday's, and Country Inns and Suites.

5. **John MacMillan (1895-1960).** William Cargill, son of a Scottish sea captain, started Cargill as a grain-storage house in Iowa after the Civil War and grew it into an established grain trader. Cargill died in 1909, leaving son-in-law John MacMillan in charge of a small-business empire that was overleveraged and had grown too quickly. MacMillan convinced Cargill's lenders to extend its credit and time to meet its debts; shut down its unprofitable businesses; and relocated to Minneapolis. Within six years, he had paid off the company's debt and repositioned it for growth.

MAJOR INDUSTRIES
Manufacturing

Minnesota's manufacturing sector is a cornerstone of the state's economy. It suffered mightily, however, during the recession, declining from 340,000 jobs in 2008, to less than 300,000 positions in 2010. It has since rebounded, although not to its previous level. Still, manufacturing represents over 11% of state employment, and more than 14% of state gross domestic product. Total manufacturing output is over $40 billion yearly, and the leading goods produced are computer and electronic products including medical devices, followed by fabricated metal products and food. Moreover, each manufacturing job supports another 1.3 jobs, which means manufacturing has a strong ripple effect in the economy. In 1948, the value of manufactured goods surpassed cash-farm receipts, signalling Minnesota's transition from a primarily farm-based economy.

Agriculture

Minnesota's agriculture sector has long been a mainstay of the state economy. It currently employs 340,000 people and generates $75 billion in economic output. Minnesota's agri-industry ranks sixth in the nation and includes 1,000 agricultural and food companies. Minnesota's top five agricultural products are corn, hogs, soybeans, dairy products, and cattle and calves. Minnesota has 81,000 farms covering more than half of the state's area (about 27 million acres). When it comes to turkey, sugar beets, sweet corn, and green peas, Minnesota leads the way.

Healthcare

With world-renowned treatment and research facilities, Minnesota boasts a dynamic and thriving health sector. The Mayo Clinic in Rochester is synonymous with quality in doctors, pioneering treatments, clinical trials, and research. Nearly a half-million people from around the world come to the Mayo Clinic for medical care each year. Moreover, Abbott

Northwestern Hospital, Allina's Mercy Hospital, and United Hospital have been ranked among the nation's 100 top cardiovascular hospitals.

Bioscience

An international leader in the biosciences, Minnesota has a reputation for scientific excellence, technical innovation, and commercialization of new technologies. The biosciences include medical technology,

One Day at a Time

Hazelden was born in 1947 when Austin Ripley, a reporter and Catholic convert, set out to establish a treatment center for alcoholic priests. The clergy-only mandate was soon discarded in favor of a broader base: "curable alcoholics of the professional class."

The treatment facility was established in a farmhouse in rural Center City, 50 miles north of the Twin Cities. It soon became a beacon for addicts seeking help, and in its first 18 months more than 150 men sought treatment at Hazelden's "rehab center." Hazelden has long been an innovator in addiction treatment, and in the 1960s pioneered the "Minnesota Model," which featured a holistic multidisciplinary approach to tackling addiction.

Today, the principal Hazelden campus stretches across 500 acres of wooded land. Hazelden has three other Minnesota locations, as well as centers in Florida, New York, Illinois, and Oregon. More than 250,000 people have sought help from Hazelden, including celebs such as Liza Minnelli, Ally Sheedy, and Chris Farley. Hazelden is considered the most influential addiction-treatment center in the nation, and also engages in addiction-related publishing, professional educational, advocacy, and research activities.

In 2014, Hazelden merged with the Betty Ford Center, another titan in the addiction recovery field. The Hazelden Betty Ford Foundation is now the country's biggest non-profit addiction treatment center and operates in nine states with a total yearly operating revenue of $180 million.

TAKE 5 FIVE GENERAL MILLS CREATIONS

Golden Valled-based General Mills, the world's sixth-largest food company, was founded in the 1860s with two flour mills. Its brands, from Betty Crocker, Cheerios, and Häagen-Dazs, to Green Giant, Pillsbury, and Trix, are instantly familiar.

1. **WCCO 830.** The famed radio station is named after Washburn-Crosby Co. (now General Mills) of Minnesota milling fame. Washburn-Crosby bought the foundering WLAG-radio in 1924 and began using it to air self-promotional radio shows and commercials, among them the famed "Betty Crocker Cooking School of the Air." WCCO also broadcast radio's first singing commercial in 1926 when the Wheaties Quartet harmonized about the nutritional value of the cereal in its song "Have You Tried Wheaties?"

2. **The Breakfast of Champions.** One way to define athletic success is appearing on a Wheaties cereal box. An illustrious group have graced the Wheaties box, including such baseball immortals as Babe Ruth, Lou Gehrig, Joe DiMaggio, Jackie Robinson, Bob Feller, Hank Greenberg, Stan Musial, Ted Williams, Yogi Berra, Mickey Mantle, and Johnny Bench. More recently, a diverse contingent of athletes, including Kevin Garnett, Shaun White, Lindsey Vonn, and Peyton Manning, has been Wheaties champions.

3. **The ALVIN Submarine.** In 1962, the U.S. Navy and the Woods Hole Oceanographic Institute awarded General Mills a contract to develop a small, deep-diving submarine. Harold "Bud" Froehlich of the General Mills Aeronautical Research Labs drafted the first design for the 15-foot submarine. Since 1964, ALVIN (after Allyn Vine of the Woods Hole Oceanographic Institute) has been used

for many important expeditions, including the 1966 recovery of a hydrogen bomb from the ocean floor and the first dives to the Titanic in 1986. ALVIN is still in use today.

4. **The Puffing Gun.** There would be no Kix, Trix, Cheerios, or any puffed-grain cereal on the market today were it not for General Mills' puffing gun. General Mills engineer and chemist Thomas R. James was the genius behind the 1937 invention, which expanded or puffed pellets into different cereal shapes.

5. **Space Food.** When NASA astronaut Scott Carpenter launched into space on Aurora 7 in 1962, he was carrying with him the first solid space food, small cubes developed by Pillsbury's research-and-development department. The space-food cubes were followed by other space-friendly foods—such as non-crumbly cake, relish that could be served in slices, and meat that needed no refrigeration. From these efforts to feed astronauts came the land-based Space Food Sticks, which were an instant hit when they landed in the grocery aisle in 1969. They had the same nutritional value as the food developed for NASA and came in a variety of appealing flavors including chocolate, caramel, and peanut butter.

TAKE 5   DAVE BEAL'S TOP FIVE THINGS
A MINNESOTA BUSINESS PERSON SHOULD CARE ABOUT (OTHER THAN TAXES)

Dave Beal retired from the St. Paul *Pioneer Press* in 2006 after nearly 25 years as a business columnist and business editor. He writes a column for *MinnPost*, is a past president of the Society of American Business Editors and Writers, and has held a number of leadership positions on behalf of journalism organizations in the Twin Cities and beyond.

1. **Support systems.** Minnesota is blessed with an unusually large number of well-developed business, trade, and professional associations established to help businesses survive and prosper. Many of these organizations support the state's unusually large contingent of Fortune 500 companies, but their presence benefits enterprises of all sizes.

2. **Mandates.** Over the years, the state government has issued many mandates requiring that businesses, particularly in the health-care and energy sectors, comply with certain standards. While these mandates are typically desirable from a societal perspective, they can lead to additional expenses for businesses.

3. **Access to capital.** Many small businesses say they have encountered problems in raising equity and getting loans from banks or other lenders. Minnesota has more banks than any other state save for Texas and Illinois, but bankers reply that uncertainty about regulations and lack of demand prevent them from lending more.

4. **Permitting.** The state has relatively strong environmental regulation, but business lobbies say that has led to a cumbersome permitting process that needs streamlining.

5. **Finding skilled workers.** Even as many workers go without jobs, businesses continue to have trouble finding skilled workers. This challenge is expected to persist for years, because the ranks of workers entering the workforce are smaller than those of the baby boomers now retiring. Minnesota's educational system is better equipped than most of its counterparts, though, easing the problem somewhat relative to other states.

They said it

"Minnesotans really think they run the whole world; I love that."
— **Minneapolis born and St. Paul-raised comedian Louie Anderson**

pharmaceuticals, human health microbiology, and agricultural and industrial biotechnology. The Mayo Clinic and the University of Minnesota, one of the nation's leading research universities, are the foundation of Minnesota's bioscience sector, which creates and supports tens of thousands of jobs in the areas of research, manufacturing, and professional services. Agri-business titan Cargill and fertilizer-maker Mosaic, among other firms, are also important elements in the Gopher state's bioscience sector.

Energy

As one of the nation's top producers of renewable energy and environmental technology, Minnesota is setting the pace in the race to reduce fossil-fuel consumption. Minnesota's wind-energy sector, which ranks fourth nationwide, generates enough power for nearly 700,000 homes per year. A state law requires that renewable energy sources like wind power must generate at least 25% of Minnesota's electricity by 2025. Minnesota is a leading exporter of environmental technology goods, but there are traditional energy producers as well, including St. Paul-headquartered Xcel Energy. Xcel supplies 5.3 million homes in the

Did you know...

that approximately 36,000 people are employed in Minnesota's forestry industry? Most of the major lumber companies and paper mills are located in the northern third of the state.

They said it

Midwest and West with electricity and natural gas.

Finance

A leading financial center, Minnesota offers banking, insurance, securities, and investment services from some of the most stable and trusted institutions in the country. Wells Fargo has a significant presence in Minnesota, and is one of the state's largest private employers with 20,000 workers. Eighteen national Wells Fargo divisions, including Wells Fargo Insurance, Institutional Trust, and SBA Funding, are based in the Twin Cities. Another local biggie is Ameriprise Financial, a Fortune 500 financial planning, banking, and insurance concern with revenues of over ten billion dollars yearly.

EXPORTS

- Total exports: $20.6 billion
- Number of businesses exporting goods: 8,500
- Rank nationwide as an exporter: 20
- Manufactured exports as a percentage of total exports: 58
- Largest trading partners: Canada (29% of total) and China (12% of total)

THE BUSINESS OF HEALTH

Health care is one of the biggest industries in the U.S. And amongst the major players is Minnesota's UnitedHealth Group. The company,

Cargill Inc.

For most outside of Minnesota, Cargill is the biggest company they've never heard of. Privately owned and headquartered in Wayzata, Cargill employs 142,000 people in 67 countries. The agri-biz behemoth chalks up $137 billion in sales and other revenue annually, resulting in over $2.3 billion in net earnings. The Fortune 500 is limited to publicly traded companies, but were Cargill included, it would land at number ten, between Valero Energy and Ford.

Founded by William Cargill in 1865 as a grain-storage company, Cargill is a global force in moving crops from the farm to the kitchen table. It buys, processes, stores and transports grains, seeds, and other agricultural commodities used to feed people and animals. The company also produces food, feedstock and fertilizer, and supplies food and beverage makers with everything from meat, poultry, and oils to salt and sugar. Cargill is in the energy business, including bio-fuels and coal, and provides the industry with lubricants, adhesives, packaging, steel, and chemicals. In addition to stuff you can touch (and eat), Cargill offers risk-management, financing and logistics to agricultural and other businesses.

It is Cargill's incredible depth and reach across multiple sectors that has made it such a powerful company. It is integral to the web of processes whereby raw goods become things you take home from the grocery store. Moreover, items that the typical consumer rarely considers—like road de-icing salt and sweeteners used in medications—are Cargill mainstays.

All of this activity has made the Cargills and the MacMillans (the families were joined in 1895 when James MacMillan married William Cargill's daughter, Edna) tremendously wealthy. Several family members are billionaires, and the recently endowed Margaret A. Cargill Foundation (whose namesake died in 2006) is Minnesota's largest philanthropic foundation, reporting more than $2 billion dollars in assets. The Cargills and MacMillans keep a low profile, something that is made possible by Cargill being privately held — the family owns 88% of the company and employees 12%.

whose revenue tops $111 billion, employs 133,000 people in the U.S. and twenty other countries, and has more than 5,500 hospitals and 750,000 physicians and other providers in its network. UnitedHealth handles more than 900 million claims yearly and serves 84 million people worldwide.

UnitedHealth has deep pockets, and it needs them. The company paid $350 million in 2010 to settle a class action suit that alleged that the company had short-changed health-care providers outside of its network. A year earlier, it had settled a $50 million suit for over- charging patients. The mother of all settlements, however, was a 2008 payment of $895 million to resolve a suit brought by the company's investors in connection with the illegal backdating of stock options. Despite these setbacks, perhaps simply viewed as the cost of doing business, UnitedHealth remains a strong company and sits at number 17 on the Fortune 500.

GIVING BACK

Minnesota entrepreneurs have a long history of charitable giving, but Best Buy founder Richard M. Schulze really hit a home run in 2000 when he and his wife, Sandra, gave $50 million to the University of St. Thomas in St. Paul. This sum represented the largest ever donation to a Minnesota educational institution. Schulze, a billionaire who started Best Buy with one Edina store (then named Sound of Music) in 1966, never attended

TAKE5 TOP FIVE CROPS
BY ANNUAL VALUE

1. **Corn**
2. **Soybeans**
3. **Hay**
4. **Wheat**
5. **Potatoes**

Source: Minnesota Department of Agriculture

college. Schulze did, however, receive an honorary Doctor of Laws from St. Thomas (a co-educational Catholic institution) in 1998.

FARMING

- Number of farms: 80,992
- Total acres of farm land: 26,917,962
- Average farm size: 332 acres
- Number of family or individual farms: 70,055
- Number of partnership farms: 6,227
- Number of corporate farms: 2,848
- Total value of agricultural products: $13.2 billion
- Value of livestock, poultry, and their products: $6.1 billion

Source: Most recent available figures from USDA, Minnesota Agricultural Statistics Service

OUTDOOR TOURISM

Minnesota, famous for its lakes and forests, is a paradise for anglers, boaters, hunters, hikers, and nature enthusiasts. Outdoor tourism is an important source of revenue for rural areas. Leading the way is Lake of the Woods County ("The Walleye Capital of the World") where 27% of gross sales are derived from tourism. Other tourism-dependent counties include Mahnomen, Becker, Crow Wing, and Polk.

People

Minnesota was a multicultural society long before the word came into the language. For a millenium, several Indian tribes inhabited the areas around the Mississippi River and Lake Superior, using the great waterways as areas of fishing, hunting, and trading.

The first European contact was with the French, but they were soon to be joined by the English as the battle for the continent raged on.

The Europeans who followed the fur traders inevitably claimed the land from the native tribes in a battle of numbers and technology that American Indians could not win. As America established itself as a country, the great westward expansion would supplant Native Americans with immigrants from Germany, New England, Norway, Sweden, Ireland, French Canada, and everywhere else. Minnesota, like much of America, became a melting pot.

A 1965 change to US law increased non-European immigration, and the vast majority of current Minnesotan immigrants now come from Africa, Asia, and Latin America. Today 7.2% of Minnesotans are immigrants, with the vast majority having arrived since 1990. During the past 20 years, refugees have come from the former Soviet Union, Bosnia, Somalia, Sudan, Burma, Ethiopia, Eritrea, Liberia, Vietnam, Laos, and Cambodia.

ETHNIC IDENTIFICATION

	Minnesota	US
Caucasian	86.5%	77.9%
African American	5.5%	13.1%
Hispanic or Latino	4.9%	16.9%
Asian	4.4%	5.1%

Source: US Census Bureau

FOREIGN-BORN

Just over 7% of Minnesota's population is foreign-born and most such individuals live in the Twin Cities metro area. The top countries of origin are Mexico, Laos, India, Somalia and Vietnam.

ANCESTRY TOP 10

1. German: 1,976,223 (37.9%)
2. Norwegian: 878,744 (16.8%)
3. Irish: 612,446: (11.7%)
4. Swedish: 493,498: (9.5%)
5. English: 333,016: (6.4%)
6. Polish: 264,617: (5.1%)
7. French (except Basque): 219,664: (4.2%)
8. American: 133,456: (2.6%)
9. Italian: 132,306: (2.5%)
10. Dutch: 107,926: (2.1%)

Source: U.S. Census Bureau, American Community Survey

Did you know. . .

that in 1970, 8% of Minnesota's population claimed German as their mother tongue? In New Ulm, that figure was 41%.

They said it

"Look forward for a century, to the time when the city has a population of a million, and think what will be their wants. They will have wealth enough to purchase all that money can buy, but all their wealth cannot purchase a lost opportunity, or restore natural features of grandeur and beauty, which would then possess priceless value . . ."

— Horace Cleveland, Minneapolis Park System Landscape Gardener, 1883, on why the park system should set aside land for future parks

IN PERSPECTIVE

Minnesota attracts an amount of immigrants roughly proportional to its share of the U.S. population. Immigration in Minnesota is heavily skewed toward the Twin Cities, which receive many foreign-born people from Mexico, Asia and Africa every year. The number of immigrants from Europe and Canada is quite low. The Twin Cities are also home to a sizeable refugee population, with a particularly notable influx of refugees in the mid 00's which has since subsided. Minnesota has a relatively small population of undocumented immigrants, probably in the area of one percent of the state population, or roughly 50,000 people.

IMMIGRANTS OVER THE YEARS

	2012	1998	1988
Africa	6,074	1,731	NA
Asia	3,527	2,441	2,717
North America	971	1,048	420
Europe	975	1,354	273
South America	441	289	183
Oceania	25	35	202

Source: US Department of Homeland Security, Immigration and Naturalization Service

Did you know. . .

that on Thanksgiving weekend 2015 the Salvation Army received a $500,000 check from a Minnesota couple? The generous pair dropped the half-million-dollar marker in a bell ringer's kettle outside a grocery store in Rosemount, 20 miles south of St. Paul.

They said it

"Give me snuff, whiskey and Swedes, and I will build a railroad to hell."
— **Minnesota railroad baron J. Hill**

IMMIGRANTS AS A SHARE OF TOTAL POPULATION
- Canada: 20%
- United States: 13%
- Germany: 9%
- **Minnesota: 7%**
- France: 6%
- Sweden: 5%
- United Kingdom: 4%

Source: Toronto Financial Services Alliance, Minnesota Compass

They said it

"Some Minnesotans got mad about that movie, but while we don't use 'you betcha' in every sentence, we do use it."
— **Linguist Karen Lybeck talking about *Fargo*.**

Did you know. . .

that Judy Garland was born, Frances Gumm on Dec. 26, 1924, in Grand Rapids, and gave her first performance there at the New Grand Theater, which her father owned? She was 2^1/2 and sang "Jingle Bells."

Did you know. . .

that Minneapolis's Cedar-Riverside neighborhood is known as Little Mogadishu because of the large number of Somali immigrants in the area? There are roughly 30,000 Somalis in the Twin Cities, and Minneapolis is home to the Somali Museum of Minnesota.

Minnesota Nice

It's not considered nice to describe someone as "Minnesota Nice." The phrase which describes stereotypical behaviours of politeness and concern for others is, like most stereotypes, partly true. A survey of personality characteristics of Minnesotans showed that people in the Gopher State do indeed tend to be more agreeable than Americans as a whole and a lot less neurotic than, say, their California counterparts.

The term itself has been traced back to 1930s Danish novelist Aksel Sandemose. The writer's fictional town of Jante was governed by 11 social rules. The emphasis is on the collective welfare rather than the individual. These findings are in line with Garrison Keillor's notion of "Minnesota Nice" as another way of saying "non-confrontational."

In a recent survey, 74% of families agreed that people help each other out; 76% said people watch each other's children; 79% said, "There are people I can count on." Although Minnesotans' thrift supersedes Minnesota Nice, you are not going to get a Minnesotan to lend you a 20; they will do pretty much anything else. They will help you jump-start your car in conditions only polar bears could survive in; if you are a mother with kids, they'll help with your groceries, they hold doors open, they nod hello, and they lend you their tool belt, or their second-favorite fishing rod.

They succumb, however, to the old small-town rules that you aren't really ever from there until the second generation. Newcomers can find this extraordinarily difficult, but it is a function of time. Minnesotans are exceedingly slow to warm and open up, but once they do, that is Minnesota nice.

MEDIAN INCOME BY RACE/ETHNICITY

- All Minnesotans $58,906
- Asian $65,989
- White (non-Hispanic) $61,667
- Hispanic/Latino $41,718
- American Indian $32,153
- Black/African-American $28,136

Source: US Census Bureau, American Community Survey.

TAKE5 CHERI REGISTER'S FIVE
MINNESOTA MEMOIRS

Cheri Register is author of *Packinghouse Daughter*, a Minnesota Book Award winner and memoir based on her working-class upbringing in Albert Lea. *Packinghouse Daughter* tells the story of the 1959 meatpackers' strike that divided her hometown. Register has also written a number of other books, and earned a Ph.D. in Scandinavian languages and literatures from the University of Chicago. She lives in Minneapolis, and recommends these five Minnesota memoirs written by Minnesota authors.

1. **Patricia Hampl, *The Florist's Daughter* (Harcourt, 2007):** Hampl's earlier memoirs, *A Romantic Education* (1981) and *Virgin Time* (1992), plus her essays on memory, *I Could Tell You Stories* (1999), established her national reputation as a premier memoirist whose lyrical style is a model within the genre.

2. **Bill Holm, *The Heart Can Be Filled Anywhere on Earth* (Milkweed Editions, 1996):** As a child, Holm thought failure meant never leaving his hometown of Minneota. When he returned at almost 40, he was broke, unemployed, divorced, and unpublished. What he found when he returned was that the people who mattered most to him and had the greatest influence on him were the old Icelandic immigrants who were his relatives and neighbors in this tiny town on the western

MOVING ON

The state's population is in a continual state of flux. Typically, immigrants and people from economically depressed Midwest towns move to the Twin Cities area for work. Meanwhile, natives leave the state for warmer climes such as Arizona, as well as for economic hot spots like North Dakota. Between the moving in and moving out, and the natural rate of increase (births minus deaths), Minnesota enjoys steady, if unspectacular, population growth.

fringe of the state. Holm's tender affection for the aging Icelandic immigrants who peopled his childhood in rural Minnesota lends dignity to the daily, ordinary, and often disregarded.

3. **Evelyn Fairbanks, *Days of Rondo* (Borealis Books, Minnesota Historical Society Press, 1990).** The book that inaugurated a new series of literary memoirs of the Upper Midwest is a delightfully frank yet fond account of a vital African-American neighborhood later devastated by the construction of Interstate 94 through St. Paul.

4. **Diane Wilson, *Spirit Car: Journey to a Dakota Past* (Borealis Books, Minnesota Historical Society Press, 2006):** Combining research and imagination to trace her mixed-race family back to the U.S.-Dakota War of 1862, Wilson challenges the dominant story of this event and shows that its legacy still endures.

5. **Kao Kalia Yang, *The Latehomecomer: A Hmong Family Memoir* (Coffee House Press, 2008):** In the first memoir to arise out of the Hmong migration to Minnesota, Yang conveys beautifully both the distinctive features of Hmong history, culture, and family life, and the losses and discoveries that are the essence of so many immigrant stories.

DEMOGRAPHIC CHANGE

The white population in Minnesota is expected to grow only slightly over the next 20 years, while the minority population is expected to increase substantially. By 2035, white Minnesotans will account for 75% of the state's numbers, compared to 86% in 2005. The Latino population prediction for 2035 is 551,600, compared to 196,300 in 2005. African-Americans will likely number 454,400 by 2035, compared to 218,400 in 2005. The Asian/Hawaiian/Pacific Islander population will likely double, while American Indians will show a modest rate of growth, similar to that of whites.

AMERICAN INDIAN MOVEMENT

The roots of the American Indian Movement(AIM) were in Minnesota. In the summer of 1968, 200 people from the Indian Community gathered in Minneapolis to discuss the issues facing the community, including poverty, housing, treaty issues, and police harassment. It was a movement that would spread across the country.

In Minneapolis, members of AIM put Indian patrols cars on the street to oversee police activity in Indian neighborhoods. In 1969, AIM joined in the occupation of Alcatraz Island, and in 1973 they participated in the occupation of Wounded Knee in South Dakota. The 71-day stand-off resulted in two deaths and 12 people being wounded. After an eight month trial in a Minnesota court, AIM leaders were acquitted of wrong doing.

Since its founding, AIM has been a permanent if uneven force in Minnesota and national affairs. It has been the most powerful voice for Native Americans in the state. The K-12 Heart of the Earth Survival School it formed in 1971 to address the high drop-out rate among

Did you know. . .

that 43% of Minnesota's Indian American population is under the age of 18?

American Indian students and lack of cultural programming has since spread across the U.S. and into Canada.

Although it has involved itself in national and international affairs, AIM has had the effect in Minnesota of positioning the plight of Native Americans on the political agenda and in so doing introducing Minnesotans and Americans to Native American culture.

GERMANS IN MINNESOTA

German immigration to the United States began prior to 1776, of course. In the case of Minnesota, German immigration to the U.S. peaked during the period 1860s and 1870s, coinciding with Minnesota statehood and German immigrants looking for farm work.

Political instability, higher taxes, declining economic opportunities, and expensive land in Germany made Minnesota an attractive place to seek a new life. In 1860, 9% of the population of the state was German-born; by 1870 that grew to 20%. At the turn of the century, first generation Germans alone accounted for 116,973 people in the state.

In Minnesota today, still more than 37% of state residents claim German ancestry. (Indeed Wisconsin has only 5% more people claiming German ancestry.) Compare that to 29% for Norway, Sweden, and Denmark combined.

Except for the Twin Cities, the Swedish area north of St. Paul, and the Norwegian counties in the northwest, German settlement has been dispersed widely across the state. Sibley County, Brown County, including the cities of New Ulm and Sleepy Eye, and Nicollet County became areas of high concentration of Germans. Winona is another area in which Germans settled in southern Minnesota.

In the north, Germans settled in Stearns County, and in cities St. Cloud and New Munich, as well as Benton, Morrison, and Wright counties, making them the majority there. Also, Germans settled in such towns and cities as Shakopee in Scott County, Le Sueur in Le Sueur County, Stillwater in Washington County, and Chaska in Carver County.

The two world wars have had a tremendous impact on the Minnesota

German community. In 1917, the Minnesota state government established the Commission of Public Safety, to which it gave broad powers to investigate individuals suspected of not being 100% loyal to the U.S. war effort. In one of the most shameful parts of modern Minnesota history, it was used to discriminate against Germans or Minnesotans of German origins.

The two great wars also had the effect of diminishing the role, number, and function of the once vibrant and numerous German organizations. German taught in schools and in churches decreased to the point that today not a single church service in the Twin Cities is in German. Historians have remarked at just how complete assimilation has been.

NORWEGIAN MINNESOTA

Declining agricultural opportunities in Norway and a significant population boom there coincided with American westward expansion. Between 1825 and 1928, more than 850,000 Norwegians had fled the old country for a new life in America.

In 1905 there were nearly 115,000 people of Norwegian descent

Hermann

New Ulm's 32-foot-tall rendition of the warrior Hermann the German (the 9 AD chieftain who led a coalition of Germanic tribes to victory over a Roman army in the Battle of the Teutoburg Forest) is the third-largest copper statue in the United States (after the Statue of Liberty, and "Portlandia" in Portland, OR).

The monument, which features Hermann atop a pedestal above a cupola supported by ten columns, is 102 foot. tall. A spiral staircase winds around a 70-foot iron column up into the cupola.

When the statue was unveiled in New Ulm in 1897, more than 10,000 Germans and German Americans crowded the bluffs to pay tribute. Speakers of the day paid homage to the old country but also to the role Germans would play in the development of the new country.

Peanuts

Schulz was born in Minneapolis in 1922, but grew up in Saint Paul, where he attended Richard Gordon Elementary School. In 1934, the Schulz family was given a black-and-white dog (Spike) that would later resurface as Snoopy. Schulz's first foray into cartooning came when he was still a kid. He drew a picture of the family dog and pitched it successfully to *Ripley's Believe It or Not!* After completing military service, Schulz returned to St. Paul where he did lettering work for a Roman Catholic comic magazine titled *Timeless Topix*. The *St. Paul Pioneer Press* gave Schulz his first significant break, publishing the strip *Li'l Folks* from 1947 to 1950. It was here Schulz first used the name "Charlie Brown." Although Schultz was clearly a cartoonist on the rise, with some of his work being published in the *Saturday Evening Post*, the *Pioneer Press* dropped the strip in 1950.

The *Li'l Folks* strip was being rejected all over the place until finally United Feature Syndicate agreed to syndicate it, renaming the strip *Peanuts*, a title Schulz intensely disliked. It debuted in seven newspapers, making Schulz $90 for his first month's work.

The rest of the story, as they say, is history. The strip stands in the *Guinness Book of Records* for being the first strip to reach 2,000 newspapers. Schulz went on to win every conceivable award of his profession and appeared on the cover of *Time* magazine. He has a star on the Hollywood Walk of Fame. The *Peanuts* comic strip alone has appeared in more than in 40 languages in 75 countries, and at its height reached 350 million readers daily.

When Schulz left Minnesota in 1958 for California, he would bring with him the characters and personalities from home and they would imbue his strips with a gentleness and decency not normally associated with comic strips. In Santa Rosa, CA, he also brought with him a passion for hockey. He owned the Redwood Empire Ice Arena there, and in 1975, he formed Snoopy's Senior World Hockey Tournament. In 2001, St. Paul renamed The Highland Park Ice Arena the "Charles Schulz Arena" in his honor. Schulz died on Feb. 12, 2000.

living in the state. Today nearly 17% of Minnesota's population is of Norwegian extraction, a figure that represents 18.9% of the total Norwegian American population. Indeed, to this day, Minneapolis is considered to be the Norwegian American "capital" for secular and religious activities.

Like the Swedes and the Germans before them, Norwegians were attracted by the prospect of cheap land and other employment. They first settled in Goodhue, Fillmore and Houston counties, and later, Freeborn, Steele, and Waseca. Norwegians also made settlements in Blue Earth, Brown, and Watonwan counties, Lac qui Parle County, the Park Region in west-central Minnesota.

In 1875, Norwegian immigrants made up a 30% of the total population of the counties of Polk and Clay. Later, immigrants also made homes in Grant, Pennington, Red Lake, Roseau, and Kittson Counties. Duluth was also a center for Norwegian immigration.

SWEDES IN MINNESOTA

Despite the fact that nearly four times as many Minnesotans identify their ancestry as German versus that of Swede, to non-Minnesotans it is the Swedes they most often associate with the state. Indeed, Minnesota has double the percentage of Swedes as a proportion of its population versus that of any other state, and seven of the 10 counties with the highest population of Swedes in the country are in Minnesota.

TAKE5 FIVE COMMUNITIES WITH THE HIGHEST PERCENTAGE OF RESIDENTS CLAIMING SWEDISH ANCESTRY

1. Rushford
2. Bagley
3. Thief River Falls
4. Madison
5. Harmony

In total, 1.3 million Swedes would come to the United States between 1840 and 1930. What precipitated Swedish immigration to Minnesota was President Lincoln's Homestead Act of 1862, which brought land-hungry Swedes to the state in droves with the promise

Karl Oskar

When Swedish author Vilhelm Moberg published his four emigrant novels, his attention to detail and rigor provided a window into the Swedish emigrant experience that Swedish Americans had not had before.

Moberg himself had grown up in Southern Småland, the place from which that nearly one-quarter of the 1.2 million Swedes left for America, including Moberg's uncles, aunts, and cousins. Indeed, Moberg had considered leaving but was talked out of it by family members at the last moment.

Moberg came to America and Minnesota (in particular Chisago and Washington counties) in 1948 (he would stay in America until 1955) to see for himself the results of the emigrant experience close-up. He amassed enormous amounts of research, which provided him with the material he needed for a series of four novels about a Swedish family's migration from Småland to Chisago County.

The novels which were an immediate success and were translated into English in short order, are considered to be among the most important pieces of Swedish literature. The novels are those of a writer at the top of his game. They capture the hardships and ultimate success of new Swedish immigrants, but also the loss of tangible connection to old ways of life. The central characters of Karl Oskar and Kristina embody the push and pull of the old and new world.

Vilhelm Moberg Park, located at the entrance to Chisago City, features the statue of Vilhelm Moberg, while in Karlshamn, Sweden, there is a statue of the two main characters, Karl Oskar and Kristina. Together they represent a tribute to the great writer, as well as a nod to the complexity of the emigrant experience.

1. **Fertile:** 54.4
2. **Spring Grove:** 52
3. **Twin Valley:** 49.9
4. **Rushford:** 46.5
5. **Starbuck:** 45

of cheap land. In addition to farming, the arrival of the railroads and the ability to work in the lumber industry in the winter meant Swedes could cover their economic bases, something they were unable to do in their homeland.

Chisago County proved particularly appealing to the Swedes. The population of the county increased dramatically in the late 19th century and by 1910, 75% of the inhabitants of the county were of Swedish decent. Indeed, until the 1960s, it was still possible to hear Swedish spoken on many Minnesota Main Streets.

Swedish immigrants have had a significant influence on the state. Swedish immigrants have contributed to the intellectual and culture of the state, informing debates and taking leadership positions in Minnesota academic and political institutions.

Did you know. . .

that Éamon a Búrc (1866–1942) was a tailor and Irish storyteller who grew up in a St. Paul shanty town? *The Encyclopedia of Ireland* said "He was perhaps the finest storyteller collected from in the 20th century." The longest folktale ever recorded in Ireland—taking three nights to tell and amounting to more than 30,000 words—was collected from him.

IRISH MINNESOTA

The great Irish migration inevitably would touch Minnesota. In the 1860s, 11,308 Irish were counted, second only to Germans in terms of ethnic groups. The great potato famine was long over in Ireland, but for Irish Americans, the prospect of large-scale farming operation with all its attendant risk and skill was not something that appealed to the East Coast Irish.

But come they did in the 1860s and 1870s. Archbishop John Ireland would become a central player in Irish immigration to the state. He first formed the Minnesota Irish Immigration Society, then the Catholic Colonization Bureau. He became the only agent for the St. Paul and Pacific Railroad, effectively controlling some 369,000 acres in southwestern and mid-central Minnesota.

In total, Archbishop Ireland would take great pride in starting 10 farm towns, all of them along railroad routes from Adrian to Graceville. Another American-Irish politician, James Shields, established an Irish enclave in what would become Shieldsville. A large number of Irish

TAKE5 FIVE MINNESOTA
IRISH

1. **James Jerome Hill** (1838-1916). Born in Canada, Hill settled in St. Paul and became a railroad baron in his adopted state.
2. **"Dapper" Danny Hogan** (1880-1928). Hogan was the charismatic and ruthless boss of St. Paul's Irish Mob during the Prohibition era.
3. **F. Scott Fitzgerald** (1896-1940). Fitzgerald remains one of the country's most famous writers.
4. **Vince Flynn** (1966-2013). Flynn penned multiple New York Times best-selling political thrillers including *Protect and Defend* and *Extreme Measures*.
5. **Eugene McCarthy** (1916-2005). Born in the farming village of Watkins, McCarthy was a US congressional representative from 1949-58; a US senator from 1959-70, and an unsuccessful candidate for Democratic nomination for president in 1968, 1972, and 1992. He was also a poet.

would arrive to work the railway. Indeed, at one point almost 15% of railway workers in the state were Irish.

Although, Irish immigration would peak in 1870s, the Irish influence on the state has been significant and St. Paul became the location for Irish ambition in the state. Despite being outnumbered by other ethnic groups, many of the mayors of St. Paul have been Irish. In the period 1932-1972, nine of 10 St. Paul mayors were Irish, and the last two mayors, Randy Kelly and Chris Coleman are also of Irish descent.

Former Minnesota Gov. Jesse Ventura didn't win any friends in Minnesota's Irish community when he went on "The Late Show With David Letterman" and said that the streets of St. Paul had probably been designed by "drunken Irishmen." It is a testimony to the Irish that despite only 1% of the population identifying themselves as having Irish ancestry they still hold a place in Minnesota discourse.

AFRICAN-AMERICANS

While African-Americans make up a smaller percentage of Minnesota's population (5.5%) than they do of the nation's (13.1%), they have long had an important influence on the history and culture of the state.

Despite being admitted to the union as a "Free State," Minnesota's treatment of African-Americans has been uneven at best. Even as Minnesota was being granted statehood, legislators only extended the voting franchise to white males. It wasn't until 1868 that the franchise was extended to African-Americans in Minnesota, and even that was under some threat.

As African-Americans would find out as they migrated to the "Free

Did you know. . .

that President Lyndon B. Johnson bestowed the Medal of Freedom, the highest civilian honor awarded by the United States, on civil rights activist Roy Wilkins? In 1923, he graduated from the University of Minnesota, where he was the *Minnesota Daily's* first black reporter and editor. He served as executive director of the NAACP from 1955 to 1977. St. Paul named an event venue after him, Roy Wilkins Auditorium.

States," freedom had its limitations. Blacks were ghettoized and social and economic mobility was limited. In the case of the 1920 Duluth lynching in which three back men were killed after being pulled from a Duluth jail, it served as a reminder of a racism that lurked just beneath the surface.

Nellie

Nellie Johnson was a quiet force in the African-American community in the state for more than 50 years. Johnson grew up on a dairy farm near Hinckley, halfway between the Twin Cities and Duluth. She came from an activist family (her father was a school board member in Dakota County) and as early as age 13 she was distributing fliers for the Non-Partisan League.

One of Johnson's early jobs was at the exclusive Minneapolis Athletic Club. When the club cut the employee's wages (Johnson was making $15 a week, and was cut to $12.50), Johnson led the charge, organizing the workers into a labor union.

She would attend both the University of Minnesota and University of Wisconsin using the money she earned from trapping to finance her education there. For more than 30 years, she owned and operated Nellie's Alterations in downtown Minneapolis.

She was also the first African American elected to citywide office in Minneapolis when she won a seat on the Library Board in 1945. Johnson worked her whole life to improve educational and job opportunities and health care. Her involvement in the political life of the state and country was so complete that it probably contributed to the breakdown of her two marriages.

At the age of 82 (she died in 2002 at age 96), she told the *St. Paul Pioneer Press* that she was still very much a radical. "I've always defined a radical as someone not satisfied with the status quo," she said. "And I'm definitely not satisfied with the status quo. Sixty-five percent unemployment in the black community — how can I not be a radical?"

In 1993, Johnson served as the inspiration for one of the nameless bronze sculpture "Shadow Spirits" by artist Ta-Coumba Aiken and Seitu Jones. The statues represent individuals who contributed to the development of Minneapolis and are symbolic of persons who are far too often omitted from the pages of history.

African-Americans have exerted a disproportionate influence on the state relative to their numbers. Their influence in music, arts, civil rights, and politics have vaunted Minnesota onto the national stage. Indeed, Hubert Humphrey under the guidance of Nellie Johnson, would see the state's politicians play an active role in the development of civil rights in the nation.

SOMALI

There are roughly 32,000 Somalis in Minnesota, making the state home to the largest such community in the nation. The growth began in the 1990s when Somalis fled civil unrest in their homeland, and many came directly from refugee camps to Minneapolis. Most of Minnesota's Somali residents are Sunni Muslim. Other African countries with significant populations in Minnesota are Liberia, Sudan, and Eritrea.

HMONG

Minnesota's Asian population also grew rapidly in the 1990s. The Hmong, who lived in the mountainous regions of Southeast Asia, started arriving in the United States after the Vietnam War. Because the Hmong helped the Americans during the war, they were persecuted when the war was over. The United States worked to resettle these people starting in the late 1970s. Currently, the largest urban Hmong population in the world outside of Asia resides in St. Paul. Revenue generated from Hmong businesses, as well as improvements stemming from Hmong investing in their communities, has improved several parts of the Twin Cities area.

LATINO

Since 1990, the state's Latino population has nearly quadrupled, and now stands at around 265,000 people. Many Latinos are not immigrants, but are second-generation Minnesotans. Mexico is the most common country of origin, but there are Latinos in Minnesota from a range of countries in the Americas and the Caribbean. Compared to other immigrant populations, which have tended to cluster in and around the Twin Cities, Latinos are spread more evenly across the state.

LGBT

Minneapolis is home to the second-largest per-capita LGBT (Lesbian, Gay, Bi-Sexual, and Trans-Gender) population in the nation (and the third-largest concentration of same-sex couples). In 1991, Minneapolis allowed same-sex couples to register as domestic partners, and in 1993 Minnesota banned discrimination on the basis of sexual orientation or gender identity.

In 2013 gay marriage was legalized in Minnesota; this followed a 2012 vote by voters rejecting an amendment to the state constitution which would have banned same-sex marriage. Prior to this, there had been a number of attempts to craft laws preventing same-sex marriage.

Gay marriage or not, the Twin Cities have been marketing themselves as a gay destination for some time. The Pride Festival began as a small picnic in 1972 and is now one of the largest pride-fests in the world, with a parade attracting some 300,000 people and festivities lasting throughout the month of June.

The Twin Cities have defined gay neighborhoods, and a nightlife that is both dynamic and welcoming. Gay neighborhoods include the area surrounding Loring Park, although many gay and lesbian people have migrated to more residential neighborhoods such as Bryn Mawr and Whittier. Minneapolis LGBT friendly bars include The Saloon, The Bolt, the Gay 90s and the Minneapolis Eagle. The oldest gay bar in the city is 19 Bar. Saint Paul's oldest gay bar is The Town House, which includes karaoke and drag shows.

Politics

Minnesotans are nothing if not reliable. The state's liberal election-day registration law has helped Minnesota top the nation in voter turnout. Typically, over three-quarter of eligible Minnesota voters cast ballots in a presidential election. Nationwide, the figure is less than 60%.

Minnesota has two major political parties: Republican and Democratic-Farmer-Labor (DFL). The latter was born in 1944, when former vice-president and US Sen. Hubert Humphrey orchestrated the merger of the Minnesota Democratic Party and the Farmer Labor Party. About 42% of Minnesotans identify as Democrats, while 32% call themselves Republicans. Independent and third-party voters make up the remaining quarter of the electorate.

Minnesotans have flirted with third-party candidates over the years, and in 1998 they shocked the nation by choosing former pro wrestler and Independence Party candidate Jesse Ventura as the state's 38th governor. Ventura served only one term, however, before opting not to run for re-election. Despite its location in the middle of the country, Minnesota has produced more than its fair share of nationally renowned political figures. In the 1930s, populist Gov. Floyd B. Olson was entreated to run a third-party campaign against Franklin D. Roosevelt. Minnesota Gov. Orville Freeman nominated John F. Kennedy for president at the 1960 Democratic National Convention, and would later serve as US Secretary of Agriculture. Hubert Humphrey served as Lyndon B. Johnson's vice-president. Humphrey's opponent in the 1968 race for the Democratic Party nomination was another Minnesotan, US Sen. Eugene McCarthy. One of Humphrey's protégés, Walter Mondale, served as a US senator from Minnesota, was vice-president under Jimmy Carter, and went on to be the Democratic Party's standard-bearer in 1984 against Ronald Reagan. Since 1976, the majority of Minnesota voters have cast their ballots for Democratic presidential candidates. Minnesota is the only state that did not vote for Ronald Reagan in either of his presidential campaigns, in part because native son Mondale was on the ticket each time.

CURRENT ADMINISTRATION
- Governor: Mark Dayton
- Political party: Democratic Farmer Labor (DFL)
- First elected: November 2010
- Term expires: January 2019
- Legislature: 88th
- Lt. governor: Tina Smith, DFL
- Secretary of state: Steve Simon, DFL

Did you know. . .

that Minneapolis mayor Betsy Hodges is a huge Wonder Woman fan? Hodges cut the ribbon at the 2014 Wizard World Comic Con in Minneapolis, which was attended by nearly 100,000 people. The mayor has an extensive collection of Wonder Woman memorabilia.

Did you know. . .

that former Minnesota Gov. Harold Stassen has run for president of the United States eight times?

They said it

"Until you've hunted man, you haven't hunted yet."
— **Gov. Jesse Ventura to *Star Tribune* columnist Dennis Anderson after he wrote that Ventura didn't understand the importance of the state's natural resources**

SENATE
- Number of senators: 67
- DFL: 39
- Republicans: 28
- Senate president: Sandra Pappas, DFL
- Senate majority leader: Thomas Bakk, DFL
- Senate minority leader: David Hann, Republican

SHUTDOWN

In 2013, the United States federal government shutdown. This was nothing new for Minnesotans, who had endured their own government closure two years earlier.

For nearly three weeks in July 2011, Minnesota's government shutdown. "Critical core functions" such as public health and safety, medical services, benefit payments and vital financial and security functions were not affected, but plenty of other things were. Thousands of state employees were laid off, vacationers were turned away from state parks (and highway rest areas), road construction came to a halt, DMV services were curtailed, and the Minnesota Historical Society closed.

The crisis arose when DFL Gov. Mark Dayton and Republicans could not agree on a two-year budget. Dayton proposed a budget with a tax hike on high-income Minnesotans to close a budget deficit inherited from the previous administration. Republicans were opposed to tax increases of any kind and wanted spending cuts. A $34 billion dollar budget, which cut services and programs, but included no tax increases, was passed. Dayton vetoed it, and the stalemate began.

Two weeks into the shutdown a compromise was reached, and on July 20, 2011 a budget was signed. Neither side was happy with the

The Greatest Show on Earth

There have been other entertainers-turned-politicos. Circus impresario P.T. Barnum proved mayoral material for Bridgeport, Connecticut. Ronald Reagan left behind Bonzo for the Oval Office. And Arnold Schwarzenegger transformed himself from Terminator to two-term governor of California.

Still, America laughed in 1998 when Jesse "The Body" Ventura plucked Minnesota's gubernatorial title from the hands of two veteran politicians, Hubert H. "Skip" Humphrey III and Norm Coleman. Sandwiched between Republican Governors Arne Carlson and Tim Pawlenty, Ventura, a political independent, was the biting horseradish in this otherwise-starchy political fare. Then, just as things were getting back to Minnesota so-so, in 2008, satirist Al Franken narrowly defeated incumbent Republican Norm Coleman by 312 votes after a mandatory statewide manual recount. That gave Coleman the distinction of losing political races to a former pro wrestler and a former comedian. More stunning than Ventura and Franken's collective lack of political prowess, however, are the real-life parallels of this political odd couple.

NAME	JESSE "THE BODY" VENTURA	AL FRANKEN, FUNNYMAN
BORN	James George Janos 1951 in Minneapolis	Alan Stuart Franken 1951 in St. Louis Park
FAMILY LIFE	Married with a daughter and son	Married with a daughter and son
PAST LIFE	Pro wrestler	Amateur wrestler
POLITICAL STUNT	Trounced politico powerhouses Hubert H. Humphrey and Norm Coleman and was elected the state's 38th governor.	Eked out a gubernatorial win against incumbent Norm Coleman after a statewide recount.
MAYOR'S CHAIR	Mayor of Brooklyn Park, 1991-95	Voice for Mayor McCheese in the 2001 TV episode *Clerks: Uncensored*

RULING IN HIS FAVOR	Sued Titan Sports in 1991 for misappropriation of publicity rights and was awarded $801,333 in royalties.	A lawsuit by Fox News claiming copyright infringement of its slogan "Fair and Balanced" A lawsuit by Fox News was dismissed but was credited with boosting sales of Franken's book, *Lies and the Lying Liars Who Tell Them*
AUTHOR	*American Conspiracies: Lies, Lies, and More Dirty Lies That the Government Tells Us*	*Lies and the Lying Liars Who Tell Them: A Fair and Balanced Look at the Right*
ON AIR	Radio call-in shows on KFAN and KSTP, from 1995–1998	Radio Talk-show host of *The Al Franken Show*, from 2004–07
BOOB TUBE	Co-hosted *Saturday Night's Main Event* from 1985–1992.	Satirist, longtime writer/ performer for *Saturday Night Live*
SILVER SCREEN	*Predator*, 1987. Ventura plays a commando fighting guerillas in Central America.	*The Manchurian Candidate*, 2004 remake. Franken plays a TV correspondent during a presidential convention.
IN CHARACTER	Appears as the voice of a self-help guru in *The Ringer* trying to boost confidence in Johnny Knoxville.	Plays *SNL*'s Stuart Smalley, an insecure 12-step self-help guru.
FAMOUS QUOTE	*"I ain't got time to bleed."* —Commando Blain in *Predator*	*"I'm good enough, I'm smart enough, and doggone it, people like me."* — *SNL* self-help guru Stuart Smalley
SIX DEGREES OF KEVIN BACON	Ventura was in *Predator* with Arnold Schwarzenegger, who was in *Batman Forever* with Val Kilmer, who was in *True Romance* with Christian Slater, who was in *Murder in the First* with Kevin Bacon.	Franken was among the original writers for *Saturday Night Live* as was Dan Aykroyd, who played one of two Czechoslovakian brothers in *SNL*'s long-playing "Wild and Crazy Guys" sketch with Steve Martin, who starred in *Novocaine* with Kevin Bacon.

outcome, and leaders from both parties heard cries of "sell out" from their more fervent supporters. The government shutdown was ugly and clearly had to end; still, by most accounts, the issues underlying it were not tackled.

HOUSE OF REPRESENTATIVES
Number of House members: 134
Republicans: 72
DFL: 62
Number of women: 44

TAKE5 AL QUIE'S FIVE SECRETS
TO GETTING ELECTED
(As told to Ruth Weleczki)

Former Republican Gov. Al Quie (1979-83) knows what it feels like to be on the outs. In the 1970s it was the Democrats who had a stronghold at the state Capitol and in Minnesota's congressional delegation. Quie's triumph marked the beginning of a Republican comeback in Minnesota.

1. **Trust.** To gain my party's nomination, I met individually with Republican legislators. Then, after I was elected, I made a point of doing the same with Democrats, believing that people would vote with me out of respect, even if they disagreed.

2. **Forgiveness.** During Minnesota's fiscal crisis of 1981, I frequently found myself locked in combat with DFL Majority Leader Roger Moe, my chief nemesis. My relationship with him changed at a fundraising event for Concordia College, where instead of talking about the economy, I spoke of the Holy Spirit. When Moe came up to shake hands, I sensed something had changed. Years later, Moe showed me the prayer he'd written in long-hand that morning on my behalf. Today, he is one of my closest friends.

3. **Ideas.** Ideas give people the sense that life will get better, that there's reason to hope. Whoever can connect with people on that

Newly elected members: 26
House speaker: Kurt Daudt
Majority leader: Joyce Peppin
Minority leader: Paul Thissen
Term: two years

WOMEN IN OFFICE

After Coya Knutson made Minnesota history as the state's first woman elected to the U.S. House of Representatives in 1955, it was more than four decades before another Minnesota woman would be

level will win an election. I offer up examples from two well-known Minnesota Democrats: the late US Sen. Paul Wellstone and the late Gov. Rudy Perpich, who succeeded me. Wellstone had a passion for people without power, and the legislation he backed had those people in mind. Perpich opened up Minnesota's education system, allowing high school students to enroll in college-level courses, with the bill picked up by the state's education department. I liked the idea so much I testified in favor of the bill, which raised eyebrows among fellow Republicans. I stood against his party when I believed that that was the right thing to do.

4. **Courage.** I ran on a no-tax pledge, but in 1981 as the state's economy slumped, I ultimately saw a need to impose some taxes. Partly because of that broken promise to voters, I chose not to run for re-election.

5. **Understanding.** I've been an avid horseman from an early age, and worked with many difficult horses over the years. The key: gain their trust and understanding through communicating. I was one of the first horse whisperers, a skill I applied to people as well. I listened with more than my ears.

TAKE 5 DANE SMITH'S FIVE SIGNIFICANT
EVENTS IN MINNESOTA POLITICS

Dane Smith spent 30 years as a writer for the *Star Tribune* and *Pioneer Press*, where he delved into state, local, and federal governments and politics. He is now president of Growth and Justice, a progressive research organization that focuses on economics and state and local budget issues.

1. **1990: Everybody Out of the Pool.** The 1990 election may never be topped for scandal and soap opera drama. Allegations two weeks before Election Day from two young women, charging that Republican gubernatorial candidate Jon Grunseth sexually harassed them as teenagers at a swimming pool party a decade earlier, throw the gubernatorial and the Senate race into chaos. Continuing allegations of womanizing force Grunseth to withdraw days before the election. Amazingly, his Supreme Court-chosen replacement, moderate Republican Arne Carlson, wins the election (perhaps the only major candidate in American history to lose a primary and win a general election) over two-term Gov. Rudy Perpich. The reverberations help Paul Wellstone unseat popular two-term GOP Sen. Rudy Boschwitz, who blunders by issuing a last-minute letter to Jewish voters, accusing Wellstone, a fellow Jew, of failing to properly observe his faith.

2. **1998: The "Body" Politic.** In a spectacularly shocking upset that puts him on the cover of *Time* magazine and propels him to instant international celebrity status, former professional wrestler Jesse "The Body" Ventura wins a close three-way race for governor in 1998 as the Independence Party candidate. His one term in office is filled with controversy, outrageous statements, and gaffes, and is mostly dominated by his efforts to moonlight as celebrity author and football commentator. Overshadowed are policy impacts, such as gains in light-rail construction and a large increase in state funding of local school district costs. He serves one term and leaves politics to pursue a career as a second-tier media celebrity.

3. **2002: Wellstone's Life and Death.** An unlikely college professor and a fiery populist progressive known mostly for protest movements, Paul Wellstone wins a stunning upset election in 1990, surprises his critics by becoming a respected and effective senator, wins re-election in 1996 despite unpopular anti-war stances and the Senate's most liberal voting record, briefly runs for president, and dies in a plane crash with family members and campaigners just 10 days before an election for this third term. A memorial service days before the election is too long and too political and is blamed for the defeat of his last-minute replacement, Walter F. Mondale, and the election of Republican Norm Coleman.

4. **2008: Enter Franken, Stage Left.** Al Franken, a charter member of the *Saturday Night Live* cast in the 1970s and later a liberal Democratic talk-radio star, challenges Republican Sen. Norm Coleman, who a decade earlier had converted from Democrat to Republican, and wins one of the all-time closest races in US Senate history. But it takes a record eight months to count the votes. The recount and court challenges put Franken in the Senate in mid-summer of 2009.

5. **2010: Rise of Pawlenty.** Gov. Tim Pawlenty, having never achieved a majority vote in either of his gubernatorial elections, emerges as a leading candidate for the 2012 Republican presidential nomination. Pawlenty, a no-new-taxes fiscal conservative and staunch social conservative, dominates Minnesota policy and politics for a decade, despite being distinctly at odds with Minnesota's moderate-to-liberal political tradition. Through vetoes and unilateral unallotment power, Pawlenty drives a historic downsizing of the state's previously expansive public sector and steep declines in tax rates. The lawyer and son of blue-collar parents presents a folksy, neighborly style and an articulate command of policy and conservative messaging. He becomes a finalist for the VP choice in 2008 and by early 2010 is raising more money than better-known competitors.

TAKE5 LEADING FIVE OCCUPATIONS
OF STATE SENATORS

1. **Law:** 18%
2. **Business:** 15%
3. **Communication:** 9%
4. **Legislators:** 7%
5. **Farming:** 7%

elected to Congress. Betty McCollum, who represents Minnesota's 4th District, was elected in 2000. In 2006, Amy Klobuchar became the first Minnesota woman elected to the U.S. Senate and Michele Bachmann the first Republican woman from Minnesota elected to the U.S. House.

In 1984, the Minnesota Legislature ordered that all gender-specific pronouns be removed from the state laws. After two years of work, the rewritten laws were adopted. Only 301 of 20,000 pronouns were feminine. "His" was changed 10,000 times and "he" was changed 6,000 times.

Did you know. . .

that in 2013 the legislature passed a law increasing the governor's $120,303 yearly salary by three percent in 2015 and another three percent in 2016, bringing the annual pay packet to $127,629? The governor's salary had remained unchanged since the 1990s. The next highest paid state officer is the attorney general, who earns $121,248, or 95% of the governor's salary.

Did you know. . .

that the Minnesota Senate offers a pronunciation guide, to ensure that Kevin Dahle is called "Doll" and Michael Jungbauer hears "JUNG-Bower," not YOUNG-bower? Others include Tom Anzelc (AN-zles), Mark Buesgens (BISK-ens) and Jean Wagenius (wa-GHEEN-yus).

Switch-Hitters

An unofficial list of politicians who made the party jump.

1857: Ignatius Donnelly, the father of the Populist and third-party movements and bearing perhaps the most prolific list of party affiliations, was at one time a member of these parties: Democrat, Republican, Independent (Anti-monopoly), Populist, Liberal Republican, the Grangers, the Greenbackers, Farmers' Alliance.

1917: C.A. Lindbergh (the senior Lindbergh) served as US representative from 1907 to 1917 and left the Republican Party for the Non-Partisan League Party for the Progressive Republican Party. He died during his campaign for governor on the Farmer-Labor ticket.

1941: US Sen. Henrik Shipstead switched from the Farmer-Labor Party to the Republican Party.

1996: St. Paul Mayor Norm Coleman switched from Democrat to Republican.

2000: Dean Johnson, former GOP state Senate minority leader and future DFL state Senate majority leader, left the Republican Party for the DFL.

2000: State auditor Judi Dutcher left behind the Republicans to join the Democrats.

2000: Gov. Jesse Ventura dropped the Reform Party, along with most of his supporters, to re-found the Independence Party of Minnesota.

2002: Tim Penny, a member of Congress from Minnesota (1983-95) abandoned the DFL to join the Independence Party of Minnesota to run for governor.

2002: Former Minnesota Gov. Arne Carlson announced he no longer considered himself a Republican due to the Republican Party of Minnesota's shift to the right on social issues. Carlson has not held elected office since 1999.

2007: Edina Mayor James Hovland became a DFL convert, leaving his lifelong Republican past behind.

2007: Ron Erhardt, a nine-term Republican state representative, converted to an Independent during his 10th-term run.

SALARIES

Minnesota legislators earn $31,140 annually, and haven't had a raise since 1999. Their per diems, however, can boost their income by more than 50%. Senators are entitled to $96 a day in expenses, while House members get a $77 chit. No receipts are required.

A salary of $31,140 seems like pocket change compared to the annual compensation of California lawmakers, who earn $116,000, plus $107 in daily expenses. But take heart Minnesota legislators:

Bio COYA KNUTSON: first Minnesota woman to serve in Congress

She is best remembered for the "Coya, Come Home" scandal during her bid for re-election to the U.S. House of Representatives in 1958. But it was Coya Knutson's fortitude and foresight and her refusal to back down that deserve recognition.

Cornelia Genevive Gjesdal grew up on a farm in North Dakota. After graduating from college, she moved to Minnesota and married Andy Knutson. To escape the abuse of her alcoholic husband she immersed herself in politics and in 1950 won a seat in the Minnesota House of Representatives, where she helped struggling farmers dissatisfied with the Eisenhower administration's agriculture policies.

She set her sights on the U.S. House, but the DFL wanted a more sophisticated candidate than Knutson, who sang and played accordion at campaign events. Without her party's backing, Knutson personally financed her campaign, overwhelmingly winning a five-way primary. In the general election, she challenged six-term incumbent Republican Harold Hagen. Knutson traveled more than 25,000 miles to the district's 15 counties, some days giving a dozen speeches. She favored farm supports and higher price levels. Her surprise defeat of Hagen made her the first Minnesota woman to serve in Congress.

During her four years in the House, Knutson authored 61 bills, 24 of which addressed agricultural issues. Education policy proved Knutson's greatest feat, however. She authored legislation that established the federal student financial aid program.

your fellow lawmakers in New Hampshire earn $100 a year, and that salary is not per diem padded.

Minnesota judges are well compensated for their labors: the chief justice earns $172, 012 annually, and the six other justices $156,375 each. Court of appeals justices take home $147,346, while district court judges receive $138,318 yearly.

Knutson's relationship with the DFL was further strained in 1956 when Knutson endorsed Tennessee Sen. Estes Kefauver as a candidate for US president over the party favorite, former Illinois Gov. Adlai Stevenson. Incensed DFL leaders refused to endorse Knutson for a third term, forcing her to run in the primary. At the urging of DFL leaders, Knutson's estranged husband signed a letter imploring her to leave Congress and return to the "happy home we once enjoyed." The letter, which focused on Knutson's "abandonment" of family, became national fodder and overshadowed the campaign. Despite a public statement from her husband admitting he had not written the letter, Knutson lost her seat in Congress.

Knutson filed a formal complaint with the Special House Elections Subcommittee, arguing she was the victim of conspiracy between her husband, DFL opponents, and associates of her opponent, Odin E. Langen. The committee ruled that the DFL antics contributed to Knutson's defeat but that there was no proof of Langen's involvement. Knutson persevered. In 1960 she again edged out the DFL's handpicked candidate in the September primary. But she lost to Langen again in the general election.

President John F. Kennedy appointed Knutson the liaison officer for the Department of Defense in the Office of Civil Defense, where she served from 1961 to 1970. In 1962, she divorced her husband. Knutson made her final run for Congress in 1977, but lost the DFL Party nomination in a special election primary. She died Oct. 10, 1996, at the age of 82.

WHERE THE CASH GOES
- Total Spending: $62.9 billion
- Health & human services: 40%
- K-12 education: 27.3 %
- Transportation: 9.6%
- Property tax aids & credits: 4.4%
- Higher education: 4.2%
- Public safety: 3.7%
- Environment, natural resources & agriculture: 3.2%

TAKE5 CAROL CONNOLLY'S EVENTS
FROM A LIFE IN POLITICS

Long before she was named St. Paul's first poet laureate and received the Minnesota Book Awards Kay Sexton award, Carol Connolly was in the vanguard of politically active Minnesota women. Born in St. Paul in 1934, the mother of eight cut her teeth on politics during the peace movement of the '60s and worked on Sen. Eugene McCarthy's 1968 bid for the presidency. Connolly's devotion to the women's movement made her no less passionate about writing poetry—even if she happened upon it by accident at the age of 40. The fiction-writing class at The Loft was filled, so she opted for poetry, which opened a new world to her.

1. **Women's Movement.** The women's movement was my springboard to the future. During the peace movement, I realized women were doing all the work but not being heard.

2. **Minnesota Women's Political Caucus.** I founded and co-chaired the Minnesota Women's Political Caucus. The goal was to increase the number of elected and appointed women in office. Seven years later, the first woman was appointed to the Minnesota Supreme Court.

3. **Women on the Bench.** In 1977, a group of women convinced Gov. Rudy Perpich that it was time to appoint a woman to the all-male

- State government: 2.5%
- Economic development: 2.1%

Source: Minnesota Management & Budget

They said it

"A politics that is not sensitive to the concerns and circumstances of people's lives, a politics that does not speak to and include people, is an intellectually arrogant politics that deserves to fail."

— Paul Wellstone (1944-2002) U.S. Senator from Minnesota from 1991-2002.

Minnesota Supreme Court. Rosalie Wahl, who served until 1994, was the first of many. Perpich appointed more women to the bench than had been appointed by all the previous Minnesota governors combined.

4. **St. Paul Human Rights Commission**. In 1977, I became the first woman and first white person to chair the St. Paul Human Rights Commission, where I served for nine years. The appointment so upset the black community that I was labeled "the shock of Nazi feminism." During one commission meeting, several men from the black community sat in the front row holding big sheets of white paper that they rattled and rattled and rattled hoping to intimidate me. I plowed through all the same. The next appointment was a black woman, not man. Progress, indeed.

5. **Wonder Woman Foundation.** When the superhero turned 40 in 1981, DC Comics Publisher Jenette Kahn created the Wonder Woman Foundation to help women who were over 40—and without super powers—realize their dreams. I was a writer for the New York-based foundation, which gave out more than $350,000 in grants to women who epitomized the virtues of the DC heroine: women who take risks, pursue equality and truth, strive for peace, and help other women.

SMOKIN'

In May 1998, after a 15-week trial, the State of Minnesota and Blue Cross and Blue Shield reached a historic settlement in their lawsuit

HHH

When Minnesota elected Hubert Humphrey to the U.S. Senate in 1948 on the Democratic Farmer Labor (DFL) ticket, he became the first Democrat elected since the Civil War. Prior to that, he had won the seat of mayor of Minneapolis in the largest victory up to that time.

Humphrey's politics were rooted in the Great Depression of the 1930s. His father's pharmacy business, prosperous in 1920s, nose-dived in the 1930s, uprooting the family and forcing them to change communities. Humphrey himself pushed his own ambitions to the side (he left the University of Minnesota after just a year), completing a two-year pharmacy course in six months to help his father in business. He would stay with him for seven years.

When he returned to the University of Minnesota, he did so with a sense of rigor and purpose that would characterize his life in politics. As mayor of Minneapolis, he led the charge to reform the Minneapolis police force, which had gained a national reputation for anti-Semitism and bigotry. He achieved national attention at the Democratic National Convention in 1948 with his historic plea for civil rights legislation and would play on the national stage thereafter.

It came as no surprise to anybody who knew him that he had presidential ambitions dating from the time of his mayoral election. Indeed, on six occasions during his career, Humphrey sought either the presidency or the vice presidency. He would, of course, serve as vice president under Johnson and in 1968 would win the Democrat nomination before losing to President Nixon.

Although he was one of the most active vice presidents in US history, it was in the senate that he left his mark. An Associated Press poll of 1,000 congressional administrative assistants conducted at the end of his career pronounced Humphrey the most effective senator of the past 50 years.

He spent the time leading up to his death from bladder cancer going room-to-room at the hospital. He even extended an invitation to his funeral to Richard Nixon, which Nixon accepted. After he died at his Waverly home in 1978, his body was laid in state in the rotunda of the Minnesota State Capitol and Minnesotans paid their respects by the thousands.

They said it

"The media would have you believe that the Tea Party is a group of old, white racists bought and paid for by Republicans. The Democrats shrugged off the massive crowds as fringe and unworthy of notice. It's only astroturf, they said. They were wrong."

— Republican congressional representative Michele Bachmann in 2014. Bachmann, a staunch fiscal and social conservative, was a founding member of the Tea Party Caucus in 2010, and was elected four times to represent Minnesota's Sixth District. She was also famous for mangling US history and facts in speeches and interviews.

against Philip Morris, R.J. Reynolds, Brown & Williamson. The unprecedented suit alleged a 50-year conspiracy to mislead Americans about the hazards of smoking, to suppress development of safer cigarettes, and to target children as new customers.

The largest in Minnesota history and the fourth-largest in the world, the case was settled for $6.13 billion on behalf of the State of Minnesota and $469 million on behalf of Blue Cross and Blue Shield of Minnesota. In addition, 35 million pages of long-secret documents were made public. The Minnesota tobacco legislation prompted the world's first public health treaty, the World Health Organization's Framework Convention on Tobacco Control. The treaty has been ratified by 140 nations.

They said it

"We, the people of the state of Minnesota, grateful to God for our civil and religious liberty, and desiring to perpetuate its blessings and secure the same to ourselves and our posterity, do ordain and establish this Constitution."

— Preamble, Minnesota Constitution

Crime and Punishment

1839: Forty-seven soldiers are confined to the Fort Snelling guardhouse for violating orders about visiting Henry Menk's saloon, near modern Fort Road and Munster Avenue in St. Paul.

1851: James M. Goodhue, editor of the *Minnesota Pioneer*, brawls in the street with Joseph Cooper, brother of territorial judge David Cooper. Cooper is upset because Goodhue printed a libelous column about his brother that included the phrases, "He is…a miserable drunkard…and on the Bench he is an ass, stuffed with arrogance, self conceit, and a ridiculous affectation of dignity." Goodhue is stabbed and Cooper shot during the fracas, but both survive.

1853: A territorial prison is established at Stillwater, funded through a $20,000 congressional appropriation.

1854: The first legal execution in Ramsey County, Minnesota Territory, takes place when Yu-Ha-Zee (or Zu-ya-se), a Dakota man convicted of murdering Bridget Keanor, is hanged on a gallows on St. Anthony Hill (now Cathedral Hill) in St. Paul.

1874: A new law permits prisoners to earn income from their labor.

1887: A police officer is shot while trying to break up a riot at the saloonkeepers' picnic in St. Paul.

1895: After a sensational trial, Harry T. Hayward is hanged in the Minneapolis jail for the murder of Katherine Ging, a well-known seamstress. Hayward had Ging killed so he could collect the life insurance money.

1899: The St. Paul police department establishes a 12-man patrol squad to keep the public safe from "scorchers"— speeding bicyclists. Speed limits are 6 to miles per hour on sidewalks, 8 to miles per hour on streets.

1909: W. E. "Pussyfoot" Johnson leads a raid on the saloons of Park Rapids, which illegally serve residents of White Earth Reservation, demolishing every bottle on Main Street.

1916: Prison labor is used to construct the longest granite wall in the world — more than 1-mile long, 22-feet high, 41/2-feet thick — at the state reformatory.

1920: Five years after Mrs. Isabel Davis Higbee's impassioned plea for a women's reformatory at the State Capitol (after which she suddenly and fatally collapsed), the Minnesota State Reformatory for Women officially opens.

1920: Three African-American circus workers in Duluth are lynched for the dubious allegations of raping a white woman. Ignoring the pleas of a priest and a judge, a mob of 5,000 breaks into the city jail and hangs the men from a lamppost. The crowd proudly poses for a photograph with the slain men.

Minnesota's Row With Death Row

The first white person and the only woman to face the death penalty in Minnesota, Ann Bilansky, was tried and convicted in 1860 of poisoning her husband with arsenic. The case was plagued by myriad problems, including whether Bilansky was actually guilty, as well as the reliability of evidence and witnesses. Even the prosecutor expressed concern over Bilansky's guilt and whether she'd received a fair trial. Bilansky was hanged before an audience of more than 1,500, many looking on from rooftops and knotholes.

Minnesota is one of just 15 states that can boast an execution-free status and, not coincidentally, one of the lowest homicide rates in the country. These bragging rights were not easily won. The morality of capital punishment was fervently debated for decades in an effort to redefine a law that continued to raise questions of fairness. But, thanks to the perseverance of Republican House member George MacKenzie, Minnesota in 1911 struck down its 66-year-old law and became the fourth state to govern without capital punishment.

Still, over a century after the state's last execution, Minnesota has a conflicted relationship with capital punishment. Support for the death penalty dropped to an all-time low of 42% in 1966, but rose to 80% in 1994. Public support has wavered since the 1990s, but the 2003 abduction, rape, and murder of University of North Dakota student Dru Sjodin put the debate back on the table. In 2004 then-governor Tim Pawlenty called for a referendum to reinstate the death penalty. The measure was defeated in an 8-2 vote by the Minnesota Senate Crime Prevention and Public Safety Committee. There are periodic legislative attempts to reintroduce the death penalty, but these seem more symbolic than anything else.

TAKE5 ERIC WIEFFERING'S FIVE
PONZI SCHEME TIP-OFFS

Minnesota businessman Tom Petters always seemed an improbable success story: a college dropout who parlayed a business selling damaged and closeout goods into a sprawling empire that included Sun Country Airlines and Polaroid. Still, few could have suspected that Petters' empire was a $3.65-billion Ponzi scheme, a spectacular fiction kept alive almost solely by the former stereo salesman's ability to persuade everyone from widows to religious charities and sophisticated hedge fund managers to believe in him.

Prior to his legal difficulties, the St. Cloud-born Petters lived in a 9,300-square-foot Lake Minnetonka home, and also kept a Florida mansion. Moreover, as recently as 2007, Petters Group Worldwide ranked number 170 on the *Forbes* Magazine list of America's largest private companies. Not anymore. When the dust settled, Petters was deemed to have stood at the center of the largest fraud in Minnesota history, and found guilty of 20 counts of fraud, conspiracy, and money laundering. In April 2010, he was sentenced to 50 years in prison.

St. Paul resident Eric Wieffering is a former business columnist at the Minneapolis *Star Tribune*, and now supervises coverage of local and regional news, including politics, education, and the environment.

1. **Ludicrous extravagance.** Though he was born in St. Cloud, Petters was an anomaly in Minnesota, where successful businesspeople tend to avoid flaunting their wealth. He drove a Bentley. He gave lavishly to schools and churches, and threw glamorous exotically themed fundraisers. He owned luxury homes in Minnesota, Florida, and Colorado.

2. **Fake, fake, fake.** Petters arranged loans with several banks, alleging the money would be used to finance the acquisition of high-definition televisions and other electronics from manufacturers, which he would resell at a higher cost to Wal-Mart, Costco, and other big-box merchants. But the transactions were a sham, papered over with fake invoices and fictitious wire transfers.

3. **Confess.** Federal investigators had no knowledge of the scheme until Sept. 8, 2008, when Deanna Coleman walked into their offices and laid out a scheme breathtaking in its scope and audacity. Coleman, Petters' office manager, was paid $330,000 a year and between 2004 and 2008 collected about $8 million in bonuses.

4. **Get this on tape.** Coleman began secretly recording her conversations with Petters. The recordings played at trial conveyed a frantic and at times desperate search for new investors. Less than three weeks later, federal agents raided the homes and offices of Petters and others implicated in the fraud. Five of them, including Coleman, pleaded guilty to various fraud charges.

5. **Revealing e-mails.** Jurors deliberated for 31 hours over five days before returning guilty verdicts on all counts. E-mails revealing Petters' involvement in the fraud proved more damning than the taped recordings or testimony of others who had reached deals with prosecutors.

1924: Herbert Huse Bigelow, of the Brown and Bigelow publishing firm, is sentenced to three years in prison for income-tax evasion. He had long argued that an income tax punished initiative. He had expected to be fined rather than jailed for his transgression.

1926: The Ku Klux Klan burns a cross in St. Paul's Mounds Park, reportedly in response to an alleged assault of a white 17-year-old girl by a black male.

1930: A Communist Party-owned bookstore is bombed on Third Avenue in South Minneapolis, after which a mob loots the store and tosses remaining books into a bonfire.

1934: Police shoot unarmed striking Minneapolis Teamsters, killing two and injuring 50. Many are shot in the back while trying to flee.

1935: Crusading newspaper editor Walter W. Liggett is machine-gunned at his Minneapolis home after alleging links between gangster "Kid Cann" and Gov. Floyd B. Olson. No one is ever convicted.

1941: Against a background of war in Europe and bitter pro- and anti-union activity in the Twin Cities, 18 members of the Socialist Workers Party are found guilty in Minneapolis on a count of conspiring to undermine the loyalty of US military forces and of publishing material advocating the overthrow of the government.

Did you know...

that in 2007, the Minnesota Legislature established a one-time, $75,000 fund to provide reimbursement of up to $300 for towing and storage fees when a recovered stolen vehicle was impounded? Prior to this legislation, no funding sources provided financial assistance specific to victims of motor vehicle theft.

Hangings by Invitation Only

In Minnesota's early statehood days, people gathered by the thousands to view an afternoon execution. The spectacle was made more surreal by the vendors and entertainers who turned out to peddle their wares. In March 1889, the Hennepin County sheriff sent more than 100 printed invitations to a double hanging in Minneapolis. The execution drew more than 5,000 spectators; another 2,000 were allowed to view the gallows after the hanging.

Outrage was fierce but not enough to eradicate capital punishment. So, Rep. John Day Smith, an ardent opponent of the death penalty, compromised with the John Day Smith Law: Executions were to take place before sunrise, limited the number of witnesses, and prohibited detailed reporting. Despite intentions to eliminate the execution-as-entertainment mindset, the law was met with resistance. Newspapers cried censorship and dubbed the edict the "midnight assassination law."

Ironically, it was the media's coverage of the 1906 slipshod execution of William Williams that ultimately led to the end of capital punishment in Minnesota. The rope was several inches too long, so that when the trap door fell away, instead of his neck breaking, Williams' feet hit the floor. Three deputies seized the rope, pulling it to keep Williams suspended in the air for nearly 15 minutes while he choked to death.

Newspapers across the state published detailed accounts of what Williams' attorney called "a disgrace to civilization," renewing calls for abolishing capital punishment. And though three papers were found guilty of violating the Smith law and fined $25 each, their reporting ensured that Williams was the last person put to death in Minnesota. House Rep. George MacKenzie's third attempt to abolish capital punishment succeeded in 1911 after giving "one of the most eloquent anti-death penalty speeches." Today, the 35 states that have capital punishment conduct executions in private.

1945: After losing his job (as a bulldozer operator) and then his temper, Robert Doan of Mahtowa clubs to death his wife and three of his four children, then sets fire to the house, killing his remaining child.

1972: Women's Advocates open Minnesota's first shelter for battered women in St. Paul.

1974: Crime Victims Reparations Act is enacted in Minnesota, allowing crime victims to receive financial compensation.

1976: First Minnesota prosecutor-based victim-assistance program opens in Duluth.

1976: After presiding over the Reserve Mining lawsuit for two-and-a-half years, Judge Miles Lord is removed from the case because he is thought to have a bias against the company.

1977: Duluth heiress Elisabeth Congdon and her night nurse are murdered. Roger Caldwell, Congdon's son-in-law, is convicted. New evidence sets Caldwell free a year later but incriminates his wife, Marjorie. Acquitted of these murders but found guilty in two arson cases, Marjorie is now in an Arizona prison.

Did you know. . .

that the *Prison Mirror*, published at the Stillwater Correction Facility, is the longest-running prison newspaper in the United States? The paper debuted in 1887, and since then has addressed everything from prison food, to inmate tastes in music, to the morality of the criminal justice system.

The Gangster Next Door

There is no shortage of colorful yarns of the Dirty '30s and the cast of shady characters who starred in the nation's real-life dramas of murder, moonshine, and money. St. Paul's East and West Sides are gangster-rich in legends true and exaggerated. But amidst the color and noise ran an undercurrent of everydayness that did not make the history books.

Now 88, Marion (Harris) Hartwick was 10 years old the summer Ma Barker and her young grandson moved in next door. It was 1931. Marion and her family lived across from Langford Park in St. Paul's St. Anthony Park neighborhood.

St. Paul had become a well-known stopping-off point for the era's Public Enemies. Newspaper accounts of sawed-off shotguns, late-night escapes, and machine-gun getaways captivated Depression-era readers. By the time she was gunned down by federal agents in 1935, Kate "Ma" Barker was widely portrayed as the matriarchal mastermind of the infamous Barker-Karpis Gang.

That's not how Hartwick remembers "Grandma Barker," who looked like any other middle-aged woman in a print dress. Barker lived a routine if unremarkable life and gave neighbors no reason to suspect her. She kept the window shades pulled, but as it was a hot summer, no one thought it was unusual. The neighborhood kids teased her 3-year-old grandson, calling him "Johnny Bow-wow" because of his last name.

The Barker-Karpis gang was notorious by 1932, having been implicated in a series of bank robberies and jewelry-store heists from Oklahoma to Minnesota. But there was no sign that her gangster offspring were rooming with Ma. None of her sons lived with her. Alvin Karpis would later tell police that while Ma Barker knew her sons were criminals, her only part was to move from place to place as mother and sons: "What could look more innocent?"

Just months after making St. Anthony Park her home, Ma Barker and Johnny moved on. They left one night without warning. It was years before Hartwick made the connection between her neighbor—who didn't seem dangerous in the slightest—and the infamous mother of a "vicious, cold-blooded crew of murderers, kidnappers, and robbers" as J. Edgar Hoover had described them.

1983: James Jenkins and his son Steven, desperate after losing their dairy farm to foreclosure, ambush and kill Ruthton, Minnesota bank president Rudy Blythe and loans officer Deems "Toby" Thulin. A manhunt leads police to Paducah, Tex., where they find James dead of self-inflicted wounds. They arrest Steven, who is later convicted of murder.

1985: For the first time, sex offenders outnumber all other categories of inmates in the state correctional system, representing 18.5% or 430 adult inmates.

1986: Flight Transportation Corp. President William Rubin and CEO Janet Karki are found guilty by a federal jury in St. Paul of perpetrating the largest financial fraud in Minnesota's history by engineering a sale of about $25 million in stock for a mostly fictitious Eden Prairie-based company.

1986: Three Gopher basketball players are arrested on rape charges in Madison, WI. The University of Minnesota forfeits the game; coach Jim Dutcher quits in protest. All players are later acquitted.

TAKE5 MINNESOTA'S
MOST STOLEN CARS

When it comes to hot-wiring, Minnesota thieves don't target just any old (or new) car:

1. **1996 Honda Accord**
2. **2000 Honda Civic**
3. **1997 Chevrolet pick-up**
4. **1995 Acura Integra**
5. **2003 Ford pick-up**

Source: National Insurance Crime Bureau

1990: The Legislature establishes the Intensive Supervision Program, which places specific higher-risk offenders under strict control and surveillance in the community.

1992: Hal Greenwood Jr., chair of the failed Midwest Federal Savings and Loan Association, is sentenced to 46 months in prison and ordered to forfeit $3.6 million for racketeering involving the institution's collapse.

1992: Minnesota's version of the "boot camp" prison is established, replacing the camp at Willow River. The Challenge Incarceration Program is an intensive, structured program for selected non-dangerous drug and property offenders. A 2006 study of the program finds that it reduces recidivism and saves taxpayer dollars.

1994: MINNCOR, the state's prison industry program, is formed to integrate and centralize administration and sales functions of the department's various industry operations.

1995: The first phase of a statewide effort to reduce burgeoning caseloads of probation officers is funded. The State Probation Standards Task Force documents the need to reduce caseloads as the total number on probation in Minnesota reach nearly 100,000.

1996: At the federal courthouse in St. Paul, White Earth tribal leader Darrell "Chip" Wadena and others are convicted of corruption and vote-buying charges. Wadena is sentenced to four years in prison.

Did you know. . .

that Minnesota has the nation's second lowest incarceration rate? Maine has the lowest rate and Louisiana the highest.

The James-Younger Gang Flames out in Northfield

In September 1876, the famous James-Younger Gang, which included legendary bandits Frank and Jesse James and the Youngers (Cole, Bob, and Jim) rode into Northfield. The eight-man gang was notorious for sticking up banks, trains, and stagecoaches throughout the Plains states. They arrived in the riverside town on business, namely, robbing the First National Bank.

The seasoned bandits' plans went awry, however, when the bank manager wouldn't open the vault, and townspeople intervened and fought the crooks. A gunbattle between locals and five robbers stationed outside of the bank left two gang members dead and two badly injured. One bank employee was also killed, as was a Swedish immigrant caught in the crossfire on the street.

The gang fled Northfield, and a manhunt was undertaken by law enforcement and citizen posses. The James brothers eluded capture, but the Youngers were nabbed two weeks later following a gunbattle in Madelia, in which another gang member, Charlie Pitts, was killed. The Youngers pleaded guilty and were sentenced to 25 years in prison.

The Northfield Raid is one of state's most famous tales and has inspired many books and movies, including the 1972 film *The Great Northfield Minnesota Raid* which starred Robert Duvall as Jesse James. Those wanting to get closer to the action than a TV screen can take in the Defeat of Jesse James Days, which features a stunning re-enactment of the famous battle. It's a hot ticket, and 150,000 onlookers crowd Northfield (a town of 20,000 which is home to St. Olaf College and Carleton College) to watch the episode that put an end to the infamous James-Younger Gang.

They said it

"To hell with the law. I want to see the execution."
— **St. Paul resident who was insistent about witnessing William Williams'**
1906 hanging, despite the Smith Law, which limited the number of viewers

1997: Two men are killed in Minnesota; the suspect, Andrew Cunanan, is thought to have killed two more before shooting fashion designer Gianni Versace to death two months later in Miami. Cornered by police on a houseboat, Cunanan commits suicide.

1999: The *Pioneer Press* exposes an academic cheating scandal in the University of Minnesota's men's basketball program. Coach Clem Haskins later negotiates a contract buyout, the NCAA puts the team on probation for four years, and the *Pioneer Press* wins a Pulitzer Prize for its coverage.

TAKE5 PRISON
BREAKOUTS

1. **1970.** An escape attempt is foiled at the State Prison when the warden fires a shotgun at a cellblock where inmates are cutting bars. During the same incident, three officers are taken hostage and armed inmates unsuccessfully try to walk out wearing officers' uniforms. Inmates surrender after listing grievances for a reporter.

2. **1979.** An inmate escapes from the Stillwater facility by placing a dummy in his cell and scaling the wall.

3. **1982.** Two inmates escape from the Stillwater facility by hiding in cardboard boxes loaded onto a truck.

4. **1997.** An escape attempt at Stillwater is thwarted when three inmates hiding in a garbage truck are observed by the truck's driver.

5. **2008.** Staff at the MCF-Stillwater thwart an escape attempt through discovery of an underground tunnel in the facility's industry area.

They said it

2001: Nearly a month before the Sept. 11, 2001, terrorist attacks, Minneapolis FBI agents are unable to get approval to obtain a criminal search warrant for the laptop of Zacarias Moussaoui, who had aroused the suspicions of his instructors at a commercial flight-training school in Minnesota.

2003: Fifteen-year-old Jason McLaughlin shoots two of his schoolmates at Rocori High School in Cold Spring, both of whom later die of their injuries.

2005: Sixteen-year-old Jeff Weise goes on a rampage on the Red Lake Indian reservation, killing his grandfather, his grandfather's companion, a teacher, a school security guard, and five students at Red Lake High School before turning the gun on himself. A dozen others are wounded.

2005: An increase in the manufacture and use of methamphetamine leads to a boom in the prison population. The number of meth-related offenders in DOC facilities reaches 1,087 in 2005, a nearly 800% increase from the 139 incarcerated in 2001.

2006: The Legislature expands conditional release time for sex offenders and adds lifetime conditional release for certain sex offenders.

Did you know. . .

that it was Congressman Andrew Volstead from Granite Falls, MN, who championed the Volstead Act, also known as Prohibition? Ironically, St. Paul soon became a hot spot for gangsters engaged in the business of breaking that very law.

2006: A walk-away from the Stillwater minimum-security unit that results in a fatal car crash leads to use of electronic monitoring for all minimum-security offenders.

2007: Par Ridder, *Pioneer Press* publisher, defects to rival *Star Tribune*, taking proprietary *Pioneer Press* financial information with him. A judge rules that he caused the *Pioneer Press* irreparable harm and orders Ridder to leave the *Strib* for a year. Ridder, of Knight-Ridder family fame, eventually resigns.

2007: Capitol Hill's *Roll Call* breaks the story of the arrest of Sen. Larry Craig, R-Idaho, for indecent exposure in a men's restroom at the Minneapolis-St. Paul International Airport.

2013: After multiple trials, Jammie Thomas-Rasset of Brainerd finds herself on the wrong end of a $220,000 verdict for illegally downloading 24 songs when the Supreme Court declines to review her case. The legal battle began in 2005 when the "download martyr" was first sued for illegally obtaining songs by bands including Journey, Green Day and Def Leppard, among others. The mother of four has steadfastly refused to negotiate any kind of settlement in the case, declaring that she would rather declare bankruptcy than make any payment to the plaintiffs.

2015: A man recently arrested on child pornography charges is declared a "person of interest" in the 1989 disappearance of Jacob Wetterling. The then eleven-year-old boy was abducted as he bicycled home from a St. Joseph convenience store, a crime now linked to several other unsolved sexual assaults of boys in the area around the same time.

FINE, THEN
The price of fines
- Handicap parking violation: $278
- Speeding 20 miles per hour or more over posted limit: $212
- No valid driver's license: $178
- Careless driving: $178

- Fare evasion: $178
- Speeding: $145
- Small amount of marijuana: $128
- Expired license plate: $108
- Parking violation: $42–$32

Source: Minnesota Courts

JAIL BY THE NUMBERS
- Department of Corrections budget: $456.8 million
- Number of staff: 4,242
- Inmates: 8,844 male, 657 female
- Average cost per diem: $84.59
- Sex offenses: 1,589 male, 18 female
- Drug-related: 1,431 male, 215 female
- Property-related: 9,993 male, 143 female
- DWI: 615 male, 65 female
- Weapons-related: 461 male, 7 female
- Serving life sentences, possible parole: 388 male, 8 female
- Serving life sentence, no possible parole: 94 male, 3 female
- Probationers: 122,000

CORRECTIONAL FACILITIES
- Faribault: minimum and medium-level security; population 2,007
- Lino Lakes: minimum and medium-level security; population 1,320
- Oak Park Heights (Stillwater): maximum security; population 442
- Rush City: close-custody; population 995
- St. Cloud: close-custody; population 1,002
- Shakopee: multiple security levels; population 573
- Stillwater (Bayport): minimum security and close-custody; population 1,619
- Willow River/Moose Lake: medium security; population 1,210
- Togo Adult: boot camp for female offenders
- Red Wing: juvenile, with a small adjacent facility for adult offenders

They said it

"He's swimming against the tide; he's swimming against reason. He wants to take the state back to a time in its history in which, I think, the state has rejected the death penalty for many decades."
— **Sandra Babcock, a nationally recognized death penalty defense attorney, responding to Gov. Pawlenty's plan to reinstate capital punishment in 2003**

CRIME PAYS

- First-line supervisors/managers of police and detectives: $38.94/hr
- Detectives and criminal investigators: $35.33/hr
- Police and sheriff's patrol officers: $26.55/hr
- Correctional officers and jailers: $20.44/hr
- Animal control: $18.58/hr
- Parking enforcement: $15.93/hr

Source: Department of Employment and Economic Development.

CAR HEISTS

Around 23 motor vehicles are stolen every day in Minnesota, and St. Paul is the state's auto theft capital. The value of stolen cars exceeds $25 million annually. The good news? Car thefts have fallen dramatically in the last decade, and are now well under 10,000 yearly in the state. In 2005, over 14,000 cars were stolen. The advent of "smart" cars with computer chips has made swiping a motor vehicle much more difficult than it used to be. About 80% of motor vehicle thefts are cars, the remainder are trucks and buses, motorcycles, and snowmobiles.

Did you know. . .

that in 1892, 1 million pounds of finished twine were produced in the State Prison twine factory? It was closed in 1979 because it did not provide marketable vocational training for inmates.

They said it

ROBBERIES
Average value of stolen property
- Bank: $2,787
- Commercial house: $944
- Convenience store: $321
- Residence: $866
- Gas/service station: $716
- Highway: $298

Total Value of Stolen Property
- Locally stolen autos: $ 27 million
- Jewelry, metals: $12.9 million
- Currency: $11.6 million
- TV, radio, stereo: $7.5 million
- Office equipment: $5.2 million
- Consumer items: $2.0 million
- Clothing, furs: $1.8 million
- Firearms: $1.0 million

Source: State of Minnesota

Did you know. . .

that in 1903, *McClure's* magazine published muckraking journalist Lincoln Steffens' "The Shame of Minneapolis," which exposed the corruption in city government? In 1936, *Fortune* Magazine named St. Paul the best place in America to hire a hit man.

CRASHES

- Total registered vehicles of all kinds, including commercial vehicles: 5 million
- Total licensed drivers: 4 million
- Reported traffic crashes: 69,236
- Crash rate per 1,000 vehicles: 1,378
- Crash rate per 1,000 vehicles in 1980: 3,446
- Fatal crashes in 2012: 395 (256 men; 139 women)
- Pedestrian deaths: 40
- Alcohol-related fatalities: 131
- Number injured: 29,314
- Top reason for single-vehicle crashes: illegal/unsafe speed (21.6%)
- Top reason for multiple-vehicle crashes: driver inattention or distraction (24.1%)
- Most common weather condition for all crashes: clear
- Most common light condition: daylight
- Economic loss to state: $1.5 billion annually
- Most common road surface condition: dry
- Month with most crashes: December
- Month with fewest crashes: March

Source: State of Minnesota Office of Traffic Safety

WHITE COLLAR CRIME
Enron Blues

When former Enron CEO Jeffrey Skilling was convicted in 2006 of bilking thousands of people out of billions of dollars, he was slapped with a 24-year sentence and sent to the low-security prison in Waseca. Downscaling from a multimillion-dollar mansion in upscale Houston to a college-dorm-turned-prison in a town of 10,000 was a lifestyle change of massive proportions. Still, the gravity of his situation could have been lightened with a vigorous game of hoops or a calorie-burning spin on the exercise bike. After a good workout, Skilling might have contemplated his quality-of-life changes gazing out windows unobscured by prison bars.

When Waseca's institution was converted to an all-women's facility, Skilling was transferred to no-perks-there Littleton, CO.

VIOLENT CRIME
Violent crime represents less than 10 percent of total reported crime in Minnesota, and the state's violent crime rate is substantially lower than the national average. Still, that amounts to around 12,000 murders, forcible rapes, robberies and aggravated assaults yearly. Violent crime rates in the state are more or less stable year-to-year, and are substantially lower than figures recorded in the mid-1990s. Minnesota's crime rate is roughly comparable to its neighbor Wisconsin's.

BLACK LIVES MATTER
In late 2015, activists affiliated with Black Lives Matter set up camp for a number of weeks outside Minneapolis's North Side police precinct. They were protesting the recent shooting of Jamar Clark, a 24-year-old black man, a few blocks away. At the same time, five black demonstrators

They said it

"Slowly the minutes dragged. The surgeon, watch in hand, held his fingers on Williams' pulse as he scanned the dial of his watch. Five minutes passed. There was a slight rustle, low murmurs among the spectators and then silence. Another five minutes dragged by. Would this man never die? Fainter and fainter grew the pulsations of the doomed heart as it labored to maintain its function. The dead man's suspended body moved with a gentle swaying. The deputies wiped their perspiring brows with their handkerchiefs. Members of the crowd shifted from one foot to another. There were few murmurs, which died at once. Eleven, twelve, thirteen minutes. The heart was beating now with spasmodic movement, fainter and fainter. Fourteen minutes—only a surgeon's fingers could detect the flow of blood now. Fourteen and a half minutes. 'He is dead,' said Surgeon Moore. The end has come."

— The *St. Paul Dispatch*'s detailed description of the bungled 1906 hanging execution of William Williams

congregated outside the 4th Precinct were shot by four men in their 20s (three white and one Asian) who said they were at the demonstration in order to livestream it. All of the protesters who were shot survived, and the shooter was charged with rioting while armed with a dangerous weapon, as well as multiple counts of assault using a dangerous weapon.

STATUS UPDATE

In 2015 a man committed what appeared to be a run-of-the-mill house burglary in South Saint Paul, taking a phone, credit cards, cash and a watch. The criminal mastermind was evidently goofing off at work, however, and decided to employ his victim's computer so that he could check his own Facebook account. The thief forgot, however, to log out, enabling homeowner James Wood to get his name, and to make posts to the robber's Facebook page. The burglar texted Wood, and they arranged to meet so that the break-in artist could retrieve clothes that he had left at the scene. When Wood saw the thief walking near his home, he called police who promptly arrested the man. Naturally, the robber was wearing his victim's watch, just so that there would be no loose ends in the case.

Did you know. . .

that T. Eugene Thompson, a lawyer who helped draft Minnesota's 1963 revised criminal code, was convicted of hiring a man to kill his wife, Carol? Known as St. Paul's most notorious crime case, the murder of Carol Thompson rocked the couple's Highland Park neighborhood and inspired a year-long media frenzy that produced near-daily developments as a botched murder-for-hire case unraveled, implicating Thompson.

Then and Now

The first census was taken in 1849 in preparation for statehood as the number of congressional representatives depends on the number of state residents relative to the rest of the country. The first census counted fewer than 5,000 settlers. By 1860, the population was 172,000, and by 1880 it was 780,000, an increase of 350%. By the close of the 19th century, Minnesota was one of the fastest-growing states. In 1900, there were 1.7 million Minnesotans, a 40-year increase of more than 900%. The number of Minnesotans has continued to rise since then, but the state's proportion of the national population has dropped. The state's seats in Congress have waxed and waned accordingly: seven seats in 1890, nine in 1900, 10 in 1910, back to nine in 1930, and eight since 1960.

Did you know. . .

that when McDonald's opened its first restaurant in Roseville, a burger cost 15 cents? That was in 1964.

They said it

OVERALL POPULATION

	Minnesota	% of US population
1900	1,751,394	2.3
1920	2,387,125	2.2
1940	2,792,300	2.1
1960	3,413,864	1.9
1980	4,075,970	1.8
2000	4,919,479	1.7
2015	5,457,173	1.7

POPULATION DENSITY (PEOPLE PER SQUARE MILE)

	Minnesota	US
1900	22.0	25.7
1920	30.0	35.7
1940	35.1	44.5
1960	42.9	50.7
1980	51.2	64.0
2015	66.6	87.4

Did you know. . .

that the home of railway tycoon James J. Hill, which was built in 1891, was, at the time, the largest and most expensive home in the state? The 36,000-square-feet home cost $930,000 to build. It still stands on St. Paul's Summit Avenue.

They said it

"In forecasting what sort of a state Minnesota is to be, the Scandinavian is a largely determining force. It is a virile element. The traveller is impressed with the idea that the women whom he sees at the stations in the country and in the city streets are sturdy, ruddy, and better able to endure the protracted season of cold and the highly stimulating atmosphere than the American-born women, who tend to become nervous in these climatic conditions. The Swedes are thrifty, taking eagerly to politics, and as ready to profit by them as anybody; unreservedly American in intention, and on the whole, good citizens."

— Charles Dudley Warner, "Minnesota in the 1880s," in
Studies in the South and West (NY: Harper & Bros., 1889)

SEX RATIO

In 1900, more men stayed single than is the case now, likely because there were too few women. For men aged 35 to 44, the situation was the most serious: There were 138 men for every 100 women. Currently, women outnumber men in the state, but the imbalance is in the 65+ category. For the 35 to 44 bracket, there are roughly 101.5 men for every woman.

BIRTH RATE

In 1900, women were having approximately five children each, a fertility rate of 168 births per 1,000 women. After the post WWWII baby boom, the fertility rate for Minnesota women declined, dropping by nearly 50% between 1960 and 1980 to 70.8 births per 1,000. The lowest rate since 1940 was in 1996, which recorded 59.7 births per 1,000 women. The current fertility rate is 65.7.

Source: Minnesota Legislative Commission on the Economic Status of Women

LIFE EXPECTANCY, MEN

	Minnesota	US
1940	65.2	60.8
1950	68.2	65.6
1960	68.9	66.6
1970	69.4	67.1
1980	72.5	70
1990	74.6	71.8
2012	78.3	77.4

LIFE EXPECTANCY, WOMEN

	Minnesota	US
1950	73.4	73.1
1960	75.3	73.1
1970	76.8	74.7
1980	79.8	77.4
1990	81	78.8
2012	83.3	82.2

Source: Minnesota Legislative Commission on the Economic Status of Women

HOUSE & HOME
Boarders and lodgers

In 1900, an average family had 4.9 people, compared to 2.55 people today. More than 100,000 people in 1900 were boarders or lodgers, with two out of three lodgers — most of whom were single — being men between 20 and 39 years of age. Only 3% of Minnesotans now live in group quarters, compared to 7% in 1990.

Did you know. . .

that the Beatles came to Minnesota for a concert at Metropolitan Stadium in August 1965? They played before a crowd of 4,000.

Neighbors

Dorothy Molter and Benny Ambrose were two unlikely celebrities, but celebrities they were, their fate holding not only residents of Minnesota in their grip but a whole country.

Benny Ambrose was 23 when he moved to northern Minnesota after an Ojibwe army friend had told him of the rich minerals there. To make a living Ambrose began to trap, fish, hunt and guide. He loved to tell the story of running away from home at 14, throwing a hornet's nest into his step-mother's bedroom and never looking back.

Dorothy Molter on the other hand came to the Isle of Pines island resort on Knife Lake in northern Minnesota (literally feet away from the Canadian border) in 1930, a youthful 23-year-old, fresh from a nursing license she received in Chicago. In 1934, she decided to stay, and when the owner of the cabins died in 1938 she became the dutiful owner.

The area eventually became Boundary Waters Canoe Area Wilderness. Legislation prohibiting motorized vehicles of any sort as well as removal of all residences left her and Ambrose as the only residents in an area three times the size of Rhode Island.

When the Federal Wilderness Act was passed in 1964, however, the government commenced condemnation proceedings taking away her ownership of the lodge and forced Ambrose from his residence. In 1975, both Molter and Ambrose were granted lifetime tenancy. (Molter began selling her own bottled root beer to canoeists and became known as the "Root Beer Lady.")

Ambrose would die in 1982 and Molter in 1986. During their later years, they were visited by literally thousands of visitors to BWCAW. They were indeed celebrities in their own right. When Ambrose died, the Forest Service bent the rules, allowing family and friends to come in by motorized boat to pay their last respects.

For an increasingly urbanized Minnesota, Molter and Ambrose were a tangible link to a frontier life that had all but disappeared. Their passing was the passing of an era.

TAKE 5 ANNETTE ATKINS' FIVE THINGS
THAT MAKE MINNESOTA MINNESOTA

Annette Atkins, Ph.D., teaches history at the College of Saint Benedict and Saint John's University in Collegeville. Her 2007 book *Creating Minnesota: A History From the Inside Out*, published by the Minnesota Historical Society Press, takes a new look at the history of the state, and rethinks what state history is and ought to be.

1. **Landscape.** The last glacier cut the Minnesota landscape with two distinct and quite different regions. Lakes, trees, and iron ore dominate the one; flat prairie and agriculture characterize the other. The two, in combination, make the state agricultural and industrial, DFL and Republican, Finnish-Croatian, Italian, Jewish, and Scandinavian-German. Lake Superior connects the state to the rest of the world through the St. Lawrence Seaway. The Mississippi River connects the state to the rest of the world via New Orleans.

2. **American Indian Movement.** Increasingly vibrant and thriving communities of Ojibwe and Dakota people with a living and active memory of treaty promises made and broken.

3. **Traditional belief in big government.** The state's founding (1858) reflects the ideas Lincoln expressed in the Gettysburg Address in 1863: "government of the people, by the people, for the people," with the emphasis on government. Minnesota is traditionally a high-tax and high-service state that leans left on the political spectrum.

4. **Minneapolis and St. Paul.** Communities all over the state have sports, music, entertainment, but Minnesotans go to "the Cities" for Vikings, Twins, Wild, and Timberwolves games, theater at the Guthrie, classical music at the Minnesota Orchestra and the Minnesota Opera, culture at the Minnesota Historical Society and Science Museum of Minnesota, shopping at the Mall of America, education at many institutions, and more.

5. **Big business.** Minnesota is home to Target, 3M, General Mills, Ecolab, Cargill, Carlson Cos., Andersen Windows, and Travelers' Insurance, just to name a few.

HOME OWNERSHIP RATES

	Minnesota	US
1900	63.5%	46.5%
1950	66.4%	55%
2015	71.4%	64.5%

Source: US Census Bureau

MEDIAN HOUSE VALUES (IN CONSTANT 2000 DOLLARS)

	Minnesota	US
1940	$31,500	$30,600
1950	$47,300	$44,600
1960	$63,100	58,600
1970	$69,100	$65,300
1980	$105,100	$93,400
1990	$94,500	$101,100
2013	$136,043	$130,615

Source: US Census Bureau.

RENTS OVER TIME (IN CONSTANT 2000 DOLLARS)

	Minnesota	US
1940	$291	$284
1950	$262	$257
1970	$449	$415
1980	$467	$481
1990	$539	$571
2000	$566	$602
2013	$819	$904

Source: US Census Bureau. Figures are median monthly gross rent (rent plus cost of utilities and fuels)

Did you know. . .

that the Minneapolis-St. Paul International Airport sits on what used to be Snelling Speedway, an unsuccessful auto-racing venue from the early 1900s?

INCOME

Median household income, in 1999 dollars

	Minnesota	US
1969	$34,295	$33,249
1979	$37,997	$36,029
1989	$40,325	$30,057
1999	$47,111	$41,994
2013	$44,230	$39,211

Source: US Census Bureau

TAKE5 CAUSES OF DEATH

The causes of death in the late 1800s were different than those of today. To start with, there was very high infant mortality; rates of between 90 and 100 deaths per 1,000 births were recorded in Minneapolis, St. Paul, and Duluth in the late 1800s. The current infant mortality rate in Minnesota is less than 5 infant deaths per 1,000 births.

Leading causes of death in 1897
1. Old age
2. Tubercular diseases
3. Diseases of the nervous system
4. Ill-defined or not specified
5. Respiratory diseases

Leading causes of death today
1. Cancer
2. Heart disease
3. Accident
4. Stroke
5. Lower respiratory illnesses.

Sources: Fifth and Sixth Biennial Reports on Vital Statistics of the State of Minnesota for the years 1894-1897 inclusive; Minnesota Department of Health

EDUCATION

For most Minnesotans in 1900, school ended after grade 8; few went on to graduate from high school. Indeed, 77.7% of males older than 10 were gainfully employed in 1900; the comparable figure for females was 16.2%. Most children who attended school spent fewer than six months in the classroom. Despite the lack of schooling, only 4.1% of Minnesotans older than 10 were illiterate; 90% of these people were foreign-born.

Today, 92% of Minnesotans 25 years or older are high school graduates.

Source: 1900 and 1990 Census Bureau reports

The Willmar 8

In 1977, eight women who worked at Citizen's National Bank in Willmar, went on strike to protest unfair wages and practices. They received only $400 a month in pay, while starting salaries for men were $700 per month. The women were also expected to work overtime without being paid. The turning point for these women was when they were asked to train a new college graduate, who was a man, as their boss.

The women first filed a gender-discrimination complaint with the Equal Employment Opportunities Commission. They also formed the first bank union in Minnesota. When negotiations with their employer could not be resolved, the women went on strike in December of 1977. This would become the nation's first bank strike.

Unfortunately, the strike went on for two years without a resolution. But the Willmar 8 had the support of the National Organization for Women and the United Auto Workers union. Actress Lee Grant even filmed a documentary about the eight women and their story. The women eventually dropped the lawsuit. Some went back to work at the bank, but not without consequences: Some were demoted; others were bullied by fellow employees. In the end, the National Labor Relations Board did not support the cause of the Willmar 8, but the women did open the doors on the issue of women's rights to a fair wage.

Did you know. . .

that in 1889 the Minneapolis Public Library opened with its own children's department, the first library to do so?

OCCUPATION

Most common occupations for women, 1900:

- Domestic and personal servants: 34,598
- School teachers: 10,818
- Dressmakers: 8,582
- Farmers, planters, and overseers: 5,402
- Housekeepers: 4,211
- Seamstresses: 3,063
- Laundresses: 3,237
- Saleswomen: 2,601
- Clerks and copyists: 2,423

Whiskey Lore

From 1921 to 1936, going to the State Fair or to Fort Snelling was synonymous with going to see the US Cavalry horse, Whiskey. Lore has it that Whiskey was too unpredictable for normal cavalry duties, but he had spunk and intelligence and before long he was turned into the top horse for the Fort Snelling Blacks polo team and into one of the most celebrated trick horses of his era.

Whiskey was famous for his ability to jump through a ring of fire, leap over a team of mules (Nat and Snelling), and bowing, of course, to adoring crowds. In 1936, at age 25, he was officially retired and lived out his life in leisure in the fort's old cavalry stables with his old performing partners, Nat and Snelling. When he died in 1943, he was buried with full military honors. Whiskey's remains, which were in the path of the new light-rail system, were moved to a new location near the Fort Snelling Visitor Center in 2002.

Did you know. . .

that the St. Paul Curling Club, founded in 1888, is the largest curling club in the country, with more than 1,200 members? Several members have made it to the Olympic Games.

- Stenographers and typewriters: 2,416
- Milliners: 2,037

Source: *Turn of the Century: Minnesota's Population in 1900 and Today.*
Minnesota Planning, State Demographic Center

AGRICULTURE

There were 155,000 farms in Minnesota in 1900, many in the southeast and central regions. Farming employed 40% of workers. Most farms were owner-operated in 1900 (82%); two-thirds were hay and grain farms, and 12% were livestock farms.

Seed Power

When she died in Owatonna at 95, Lillian Colton was a legend in Minnesota farm circles. Although she grew up on a farm in Sherburn in Martin County, she spent 67 years running a beauty shop in Owatonna called the Clip and Curl.

In 1966 at the age of 54, Lillian decided to take part in the crop art competition at the Minnesota State Fair, entering as a seed artist using crops like wild rice and timothy seed glued to particle board to make portraits. In the first 11 years she won nine best-of-show purple ribbons. She retired from competition in 1983 to give other competitors a chance, but continued to be part of the show and was eventually hired by the fair to do live demonstrations of crop art techniques for fair goers.

There were 26.2 million acres of land given over to farming. There were 6,227 farms in Otter Tail County, the most of any county, and only 19 farms in Lake County. The largest average farm was 415 acres, on White Earth Reservation. The largest average acreage farms were in western Minnesota, which had been settled at a time when mechanization allowed farmers to work more land.

Although farming is still a vital industry, today is accounts for only 3.4% of workers. Slightly less land is now used for farming: 26 million acres. In 1900, the average farm was 170 acres; today, that figure is 354 acres.

FLOUR MILLING

In the late 1800s, technological advances made it easier to process spring wheat. Minneapolis became known as the Flour Milling Capital of the World and Pillsbury's A Mill became the world's largest mill. The mill sat on the banks of the Mississippi River and drew power from St. Anthony Falls. Across the river from the A Mill sat the world's second largest mill, the Washburn A Mill, which was rebuilt after a fire destroyed it in 1878. It was considered state-of-the-art, with new automatic steel rollers and safer operating systems. During its busiest times, this mill could crank out enough flour each day for 12 million loaves of bread. The mill was home to another well-known company: General Mills.

Did you know. . .

that Minneapolis hosted the 1892 Republican National Convention? The next time a national political convention was held in the state was 2008, when the Republicans gathered in St. Paul. Forty-five thousand attendees and 15,000 media members filled Twin Cities' hotels for the event.

They said it

"What shall the new century bring forth? ... It is not too much to hope that we shall conquer the air...and fly from place to place as free as birds... With the terrible advances we have made in the naval and military arts of destruction, may we not hope that an era of international arbitration is dawning? Shall we not look, too, for an advance in the science of human government leading rapidly to less corruption...and more wisdom in the collection of revenues and their disbursement?"

— *Minneapolis Times*, Jan. 1, 1901

Flour milling helped the city of Minneapolis grow; its population expanded from 13,000 to more than 160,000 in just 20 years. After World War I, the city's milling industry declined. The Washburn A Mill closed in 1965 and was nearly destroyed (again) by fire in 1991. The Minnesota Historical Society rebuilt the interior into a museum: the Mill City Museum opened in 2003.

THE GREAT DEPRESSION

In 1929, several large employers in Minneapolis went bankrupt, and many more followed throughout the state. When the unemployment rate was hitting 25% nationwide, it was at nearly 70% in Minnesota's Iron Range and farming communities. Farmers watched prices fall and costs and debts increase. It didn't help that, starting in 1931, a nearly decade-long drought started drying up crops and soil and causing massive dust storms. In 1933, 60 out of every 1,000 farmers in Minnesota declared themselves bankrupt.

All these hardships were suffered without electricity and indoor plumbing: farm families had never had these conveniences in the first place and didn't receive government assistance until the Depression was nearly over. Without a steady farming income, families were forced to move to the cities to find work. Mothers made due with a couple of days worth of food for weeks at a time. Children collected trash for income or found low-paying jobs, such as being newsboys, to supplement the family's income. By 1930, nearly 8% of Minnesota children ages 10-17 were employed.

In 1933, Minnesota established a district of the Civilian Conservation Corps (CCC), which gave work to unemployed, unmarried men (white, black, and American Indian) between the ages of 17 and 23. The Minnesota CCC worked to plant trees, build roads, hang telephone lines, and improve state park facilities. By the end of the program in 1942, the CCC employed nearly 84,000 men, paying them around $30

TAKE5 FIVE PIONEERING
MINNESOTA WOMEN

1. **Mee Moua (1969-):** In 2002 Moua was the first Hmong American to be elected to the Minnesota State Senate. She left politics in 2010, and is currently president and executive director of Asian Americans Advancing Justice.

2. **Harriet Bishop (1817-83):** Bishop came west from Vermont to help educate frontier children in the 1840s. She became active in teaching moral issues such as suffrage and educational reform. She started the first public school in St. Paul. The city's popular Harriet Island, located in the Mississippi, was named for her.

3. **Eugenie Moore Anderson (1909-97):** In 1944, Anderson helped create the Democratic-Farmer-Labor Party of Minnesota. President Harry Truman made her the first female American ambassador in 1949 when he appointed her ambassador to Denmark.

4. **Sister Elizabeth Kenny (1880-1952):** Kenny discovered a treatment for infantile paralysis in her native Australia. She established the Sister Kenny Institute in Minnesota in 1942. She urged that polio patients exercise their limbs, and this led to the rehabilitation therapy that we know today.

5. **Beatrice Scheer Smith (1913-2010):** An expert botanist who held a Ph.D. in the field, Smith spent her lifetime spreading her love of science to young women. In 2001, she helped found the Minnesota School of Botanic Art at The Bakken Museum in Minneapolis.

per month ($25 of that had to either be sent home or deposited with the Army finance officer). The program ended in 1942: 124 million trees had been planted, 4,000 miles of new road laid, 3,300 miles of firebreaks built, and 1,635 miles of forest telephone lines strung.

PLANES, TRAINS, AND ALTERNATE VEHICLES
Air travel

The Minneapolis-St. Paul International Airport started as a single hangar in 1920. In 1926, local airline Northwest Airways (which merged with Delta Airlines in 2008) took over the hangar for the delivery of airmail. The airport first provided passenger service in 1929 and international service in 1948. The airport's main terminal, Lindbergh, opened to the public in 1962 and exceeded its capacity by 1967. The airport now houses two terminals and four runways, and serves 33 million passengers yearly (17th busiest in North America).

Railroads

In 1830, the railroads in the US ran for only 23 miles. In 1850, states began to grant land to railroad companies to build more. In 1857, Minnesota got onboard when it granted five million acres and millions in state bonds to the Minnesota & Northwest Railroad. The first line in the state ran for 10 miles between St. Paul and St. Anthony Falls. It began operations in early July of 1862; the rails were made of iron and the two locomotives burned wood. That railway became the St. Paul & Pacific Railroad Co., which Canadian businessman and former ticket agent James Jerome Hill and his associates bought in 1878. Over the next 20 years, Hill acquired and

Did you know. . .

that after the mass execution of 38 American Indians in Mankato, William Mayo was one of the physicians who received an Indian body for medical research? In 1998, the body was returned by the Mayo Clinic to a Dakota tribe for reburial under the Native American Graves Protection and Repatriation Act.

expanded, competing with the likes of Northern Pacific and eventually creating the Great Northern Railway, which ran from St. Paul to Seattle.

The railways sold land to settlers, developing towns along its tracks; the founders of some of those towns were often employed in, or associated with, the rail industry. Industries began using the railroad to transport goods. Farmers took advantage of the new transportation system by producing foods and shipping them out to new markets. Warehouse districts had to be established to handle goods; Minneapolis and St. Paul, being hub cities, were key beneficiaries.

The airport is connected to surrounding areas by Minnesota's latest transportation venture. The Hiawatha Light Rail line, completed in 2004, runs 12 miles from Minneapolis to the Mall of America in Bloomington. The light rail carries millions of commuters each year, and future expansion to St. Paul and the western suburbs are in the works. In 2009, the Northstar Commuter Rail opened, linking the northern suburbs with Minneapolis and the Hiawatha Light Rail line.

Public transport

Minneapolis developed its streetcar system in 1875. The Minneapolis Street Railway traveled four miles through the center of downtown and 14 people could fit in one car, of which there were 10. The network was extended to Lake Minnetonka in 1882, and cruised past Minneapolis's Lake Harriet along the way, providing urban dwellers respite from the city. The streetcars began to struggle around the time of the Great Depression, and eventually ended in the mid-1950s, when private automobiles became more common and buses the dominant mode of public transportation.

Metro Transit serves the Twin Cities public transit needs today, and its buses, light-rail and commuter trains provide 84.5 million rides every year, operating 132 routes over a 900 square mile area. The Metro Green Line now connects the downtown areas of Minneapolis and St. Paul.

Thanks to the Minnesota Streetcar Museum, those wishing to

step back in time can still ride historic streetcars. The museum operates two modest lines during the warmer months: one in Excelsior southwest of Minneapolis, and another in Minneapolis along Lake Harriet's west side.

WAR, WHAT WAS IT GOOD FOR?
Civil War
Fort Sumter fell to Confederate troops from North Carolina in 1861, and when President Lincoln called for troops in April, the First Minnesota Volunteer Infantry Regiment was among the first in the nation to sign up. The regiment made history at the Battle of Gettysburg on July 2, 1863. That evening, Union troops were outnumbered five to one. With reinforcements five minutes away, the Union commander ordered the regiment to immediately charge the Confederate line. Those 262 men swept forward across 200 yards of open ground, bayonets fixed, to the momentary astonishment of the Confederate soldiers. All but 47 died, giving the Union time enough to bring in reinforcements and fight on. The survivors held annual reunions in St. Paul until 1932; the last members of the regiment died in 1936. In total, 26,717 Minnesotans volunteered to fight in the Civil War.

World War I
US National Guard members were brought together to form the Rainbow Division in 1917; Minnesota's 151st Field Artillery was part of the division, serving in France in 1917 and 1918. Nearly 120,000 soldiers and 1,000 nurses from Minnesota served during World War I; about 3,500 died. There was an anti-German movement during World War I, and the Minnesota Commission of Public Safety was given the right to bully and suppress local Germans.

World War II
On Jan. 26, 1942, Private Milburn Henke of Hutchinson was the first enlisted man to land with the first American Expeditionary Force in Europe in World War II. More than 300,000 troops passed through Fort

Snelling on their way to fight in World War II, with more than 6,000 giving their lives. Minnesota contributed in other ways as well. Gliders known as "Silent Wings," used to transport troops and equipment behind enemy lines, were produced by the thousands in the Twin Cities. And the Minnesotan Andrews Sisters were one of the most popular female music groups during World War II. They entertained troops around the world with songs like "Don't Sit Under the Apple Tree" and "Boogie Woogie Bugle Boy." In 1947, close to half of all college and university students in Minnesota were veterans being educated under the GI Bill.

Vietnam and Korea

Close to 95,000 Minnesotans served in the Korean War, with 738 killed and 154 missing in action. From 1961 to 1975, more than 68,000 Minnesotans fought in Southeast Asia during the Vietnam war. More than 1,000 were killed or missing in action. Students at the Minneapolis campus of the University of Minnesota joined fellow students across the country to protest the war. Police responded by using tear gas on protestors.

MEDIA
Broadcasting

In 1922, nine radio stations went on the air in Minnesota; three of the nine were started by newspapers, and all three stopped broadcasting simultaneously in September of that year. U of Minnesota's station, WLB, officially began broadcasting on Jan. 13, 1922. Among its early program: Gopher football games. WLAG, owned by the Cutting and Washington Corp., which manufactured radio receivers, went on to become WCCO, the largest radio station in the Upper Midwest. The number of radio stations had grown to 11 by 1930 and inched up to 20 by the end of that decade.

Minnesota Public Radio began as a classical music station in 1967. Now it operates 38 stations regionally and reaches 850,000 weekly listeners, the largest audience of any regional public radio network.

They said it

"...this extensive, rich and salubrious region would open new induce-
ments for the enterprize of our countryman; that it is not only rich in
soil, but...in minerals: that it is sufficiently timbered and watered for
agricultural purposes: and your memorialists feel a conviction that this
country once thrown open to settlement, would be peopled with a
rapidity exceeding any thing in the history of Western colonization . . ."
— **Memorial to Congress about the purchase of the Sioux Indian
lands west of the Mississippi River; Oct. 20, 1849**

The organization has won nearly 1,000 broadcasting and journalism
awards and produces successful national programming such as Garrison
Keillor's popular *A Prairie Home Companion*.

KSTP-TV Channel 5 was the upper Midwest's first commercial
television station when it started broadcasting in 1948. It still remains
the only locally owned, locally operated broadcasting company in the
Twin Cities area. It's remained a groundbreaking station by being
the first full-color station in the country, the first to offer a seven-day
newscast schedule, the first station to broadcast the first baseball game
in Minnesota, and most recently the first TV station in Minnesota to
change to the high-definition digital format.

Newspapers

James Goodhue published the first edition of *The Minnesota Pioneer* in April
1849. This paper eventually became the *St. Paul Pioneer Press*, which is
primarily delivered to the east side of the Twin Cities metro area. Today's
Minneapolis Star Tribune has been around in some format or another, with
some name or another, since the mid-1800s. *Finance and Commerce* has
been publishing business news about the Twin Cities since 1887.

In 1900 there were 677 newspapers and periodicals published in
the Gopher State; by 1910, there were 757, and by 1920, there were
761. The *Minneapolis Star Tribune* and the *St. Paul Pioneer Press*, are
Minnesota's two surviving major dailies.